Inclusive Education

For Children with Special Needs

Neena Dash

ATLANTIC

PUBLISHERS & DISTRIBUTORS (P) LTD

ATLANTIC
PUBLISHERS & DISTRIBUTORS (P) LTD
7/22, Ansari Road, Darya Ganj, New Delhi
Tel.: +91-11-4077 5252, 2327 3880
E-mail: orders@atlanticbooks.com
Web: www.atlanticbooks.com

Reprint 2025, 2020

Published by Atlantic Publishers & Distributors (P) Ltd.

Printed & bound in India by Atlantic Print Services

Preface

This book is based on research on inclusion, and it seeks to find out how information/findings from research conducted abroad and in our country can be used to influence inclusive practices in classrooms in a positive way. It is particularly written for those who need tips and strategies relating to WHY, WHOM and HOW to include children with special needs in regular classroom activities. University research scholars will also find the book quite useful for them.

Realising the value of time for modern-day teachers and scholars, I have tried to make this book as accessible as possible. Wherever possible I have tried to avoid large sections of text in favour of tables, boxes, figures and pictures so as to facilitate easy understanding of the subject matter. A detailed bibliography has been included to enable the inquisitive readers to pursue the subject further.

The present book is the successful outcome of my in-depth study during the period of my research and after; valuable guidance of Prof. (Dr.) D.S. Yadav, former Professor of Education and Dr. Sangeeta, Reader in the Department of Education, Kurukshetra University; and the material assistance rendered by Prof. M. Dash, former Principal of R.N. Institute of Advanced Studies in Education, Cuttack. I have been fortunate to get the opportunity to participate in various orientation programmes and refresher courses and to interact with experts in these programmes organized by Rehabilitation Council of India; International Portage Association, Florida;

Indian National Portage Association, Chandigarh; Academic Staff College, H.P. University, Shimla; Department of Education of Groups with Special Needs, NCERT, New Delhi; and the Directorate of Teacher Education and SCERT, Bhubaneswar, Orissa. Such participation proved a great help to me in writing the present book. I express my deep sense of gratitude to these learned experts, organizations and particularly to my research guides.

I keep on record the interest shown and the advice given to me by Dr. K.R. Gupta, Chairman and Chief Editor of Atlantic Publishers and Distributors (P) Ltd. and also the timely assistance in the form of literature provided by Mr. Manish Gupta, Director of Atlantic Publishers and Distributors (P) Ltd. for publishing the book.

Concerted effort has been made to make the book self-contained and easily comprehensible. Any suggestion and criticism for the improvement of the book are always welcome and will be duly acknowledged.

NEENA DASH

Contents

Children with Special Needs

1

THE CONCEPT OF CHILDREN WITH SPECIAL NEEDS

The conceptualization of "Children with Special Needs" determines the policy, research and practice in special needs education. The concept of children with special needs is of British origin. The Government Commission chaired by Baroness Mary Warnock (1978) reported to the government on the findings of its inquiry into special education in Britain. It was wrong, said the report, to identify children by means of their 'handicap,' and then send them to schools organized to deal with just such categories. Rather, the report went on, we should identify their educational difficulties and provide accordingly. And so the term Special Educational Needs (SEN) entered UK legislation, its classrooms and importantly—teachers' thinking.

Prior to 1944, provision of education was made on the basis of a specific handicap, i.e., visual and hearing impairment, essentially through charitable initiatives. The emphasis was more on training than on education. In the period following World War II an increasing amount of research was directed at children with special education needs, particularly in the USA. It was recognized that this could not be achieved through the classification of children into handicap categories which had no direct educational implications. Parents became conscious and concerned that their children's educational needs should be met. Parents' organizations were started which then exerted pressure to improve educational provisions.

In an effort to dispel the stigma associated with the negative labels of the past, the old language, which labeled disabled people as 'lame,' 'defective,' 'crippled,' 'less fortunate,' 'mentally retarded,' 'spastic,' 'deaf and dumb'—all of which focused on their imperfections, was abandoned and replaced by the new language whereby children with disabilities were described in broader, more general terms such as 'Children with Special Educational Needs' in the light of the recommendations of Warnock's committee.

The old disability implied a mistaken model seeing difficulties within the individual child and disregarding the numerous facets in the external environment which disable the child. The old approach was regarded as a medical approach and known as the medical model. Today the approach is a social one looking, in stead, at all the barriers within the environment that can disable a person.

Research on social deprivation also indicated that children's educational programme did not reflect factors within the child but within the child's environment. This led to the Head Start Programme in USA and the 'educational priority area' programme in Britain.

There is no legal definition of this term in India. The PWD Act (1995) defines the term disability and different types of disabilities. There are checklists available to identify the various disabilities and are currently used to identify special needs children.

While use of the term Special Educational Needs or Children with Special Educational Needs sounds very pleasant and affirmative there are certain conceptual and practical problems while making a decision as to whether a child has certain SEN. The conceptual issues are:

(a) Nature of SEN;
(b) The rights of those with SEN and their parents and
(c) The effectiveness of identifying, assessing and meeting SEN.

The current conceptualization of SEN is widely considered to constitute a major change from the previous framework based on handicap or categorization. The concept of SEN is more positive as it is concerned with every thing about the child's abilities and disabilities as well as resources and constraints in the environment which affect educational progress.

There are two interpretations of special needs education:

(a) Special needs education is additional and different to ordinary provision and

(b) Ordinary provision is not accommodating to the diversity of individual needs.

Both interpretations capture significant aspects of what is involved in the field of providing for pupil diversity. But neither is sufficient without the other. This can be understood by considering the concept of SEN as a way of resolving conceptually the dilemma of identifying and providing for diversity. The tension arises from the existence of the negative social values placed on impairments and difficulties, on the one hand, and the scarcity of provision and difficulties in managing provision, on the other. Stigma and devaluation can be avoided by including pupils into the mainstream, but that runs into scarcity and management limitations.

Of course, this is to put the tension in a stark and simple way, and there are in practice more and less effective ways of finding a balance. At present no final resolution to this dilemma is in view. This has, therefore, to be faced, digested and lived with. It means that a complex concept like SEN, despite its usefulness, is problematic. It also means that the interpretation of the concept as "ordinary provision not accommodating individual needs" is only a part of the matter. This interpretation looks forward to special educational needs no longer existing at some future time when full diversity can be accommodated. However, for as long as, and to the extent that ordinary provision cannot accommodate, there will be the need for additional and different provision—there will be educational needs in the other sense.

Children with special needs are unique individuals. Their uniqueness may be noticed in one or more of the following dimensions: vision, hearing, movement, communication, perceptual-motor, social-emotional, intelligence and adaptive behaviour. These children were previously regarded as children with diverse abilities (both children with giftedness and disability, disturbances and disadvantages).

TYPES OF CHILDREN WITH SPECIAL NEEDS

Special needs children deviate from the normal children either in the positive direction or in the negative direction. Consequently, there are various types of special needs children. They are:

- Children with hearing impairment;
- Children with visual handicap;
- Children with mental retardation;
- Children with learning disability;
- Children with speech handicap;
- Children with multiple handicaps;
- Children with orthopaedic handicap;
- Children with emotional disturbance;
- Children with superior intellectual ability or gifted children;
- Children with creative talents;
- Children with social disadvantages and
- Children with delinquent tendencies.

Types of Exceptional Children

(-ve direction)
- Visually Impaired (Blind and Low Vision)
- Hearing Impaired (Deaf and Hard-of-Hearing)
- Learning Disabled
- Mentally Retarded (Intellectually Challenged)
- Orthopaedically Impaired
- Speech Handicapped
- Socially Disadvantaged
- Emotionally Disturbed
- Delinquent Children

(+ve direction)
- Gifted Children
- Talented Children
- Creative Children

Children with Hearing Handicap

The hearing handicapped children are those children who have a damaged hearing mechanism and face difficulty in speech and language development. There is loss of hearing. The degree of hearing loss is less in some children while it is more severe in others. The hearing handicapped children may be hard-of-hearing or deaf.

The hard-of-hearing children are those children who have hearing loss but who can hear if spoken too loudly without a hearing aid. A hearing aid will enable them to hear better.

The deaf are those who can not hear even if spoken to very loudly. They require preparation in basic skills through special techniques before they are admitted in general schools. Hearing aids help them to become more functional.

Children with Visual Handicap

The visually handicapped children are those who have problems with vision. Some visually handicapped children can read large print and are functional in their environment whereas some have severe vision loss and can not be taught through visual methods. The visual loss is measured with the help of 'Snellen Chart'. Depending upon the degree of loss they may be partially sighted or blind.

The partially sighted are those who require large print or magnified print materials. Their visual acuity (sharpness of visual image) is very low (20/70 in the better eye). This means that the child can see at 20 ft. distance what a normal child sees at 70 ft. distance. Their eye-sight may be weak due to short-sightedness, long-sightedness, astigmatism, glaucoma or muscle detachment.

The blind are those who need to be taught through Braille or through aural method. Their visual acuity (sharpness of visual image) may fall at 2/200.

Children with Mental Retardation

Mentally retarded children are those who have a lower level of intellectual functioning and have problems in social adaptability. There are various degrees of mental handicap. Consequently, there are various categories of mentally handicapped children—the Educable Mentally Retarded (EMR), the Trainable Mentally Retarded (TMR) and the Custodial Mentally Retarded (CMR).

The educable mentally retarded are those who have minimum educational retardation in school subjects. Such children have problems of social adjustment, but are usually not recognized as mentally retarded at the pre-school level. They need repetition of instruction. The adaptive behaviours of such children should be observed carefully by the teachers so that they can be identified in the early stages.

The trainable mentally retarded can be trained in vocational areas. They are poor in adaptive behaviour and may need training in daily living skills at the initial levels.

Children with Learning Disability

These children are like other children in intellectual functioning. They are not mentally retarded, nor do they have visual or hearing problems. But they have problems in spelling, reading, writing, arithmetic, listening and comprehension. Their problem may be due to cerebral dysfunction/emotional/behavioural disturbance, but it is not due to mental retardation, sensory handicap or instructional practices. Depending upon the degree of disability such children may be categorized into mild learning disabled and severe learning disabled.

Such children have a severe discrepancy between their achievement and intellectual ability. Such children may have the following specific problems:

- Reading disability;
- Writing disability;
- Problems in comprehension and communication and
- Problems with numerical ability.

Children with Speech Handicap

Speech handicap refers to minor and major speech and language problems. There are children with mild language and speech disorders in our classrooms, and they often go unnoticed. While speaking and writing they tend to omit, distort, add or substitute words, phrases, letters of the alphabet, etc. They stammer and are quiet or have long gaps in speaking full sentences. Their problems should be corrected before they start school. The major types of speech disorders are:

- Voice disorders,
- Articulation or pronunciation disorders and
- Fluency disorders.

Children with Orthopaedic Handicap

Some children have orthopaedic handicap or locomotor handicap. Locomotor handicap refers to problems with the functioning of bones, joints and muscles. In some cases, the problems are so severe that they require artificial limbs to compensate for their crippling conditions. In other cases they need wheel-chair or crutches.

Children with Multiple Handicaps

Multiple handicaps refer to more than one handicap in the child. A child may be blind and deaf, blind and orthopaedically handicapped, deaf and orthopaedically handicapped, mentally retarded and orthopaedically handicapped and so on. In case of multiple handicaps, one handicap may be primary handicap and the other secondary or one handicap may be more severe than the other handicaps. It is, therefore, important to identify the primary handicap and take measures accordingly.

Children with Emotional Disturbance

Children with emotional disturbance are very often considered as problem children in the school. An emotionally disturbed child has certain inner tensions which create anxiety, frustration, fears and impulsive behaviour. Such a child may find excuses for his inner tensions in some physical difficulty. An emotionally disturbed child may attempt to solve the anxiety by behaving in a premature or childish way, becoming aggressive towards other people, or withdrawing himself to the world of fantasy.

Gifted Children

Gifted children are in some way superior in intellectual ability to other children of the same age. Gifted children are those who have demonstrated high ability (including high intelligence), high creativity and high task commitment—a high level of motivation and the ability to see a project through to its conclusion. A variety of terms have been used to describe individuals who are superior in some way such as 'talented,' 'creative,' 'genius,' and 'precocious' (remarkably early development in particular areas like language, music, mathematical ability).

Children with Creative Talents

In a school, teachers may come across a few students who have the ability to produce something new—a composition, a system of ideas or a material or a process which is essentially new or novel, and previously unknown to them. Such children behave differently. They are courageous in their convictions. They have independent thinking and adjustment. They become absorbed and preoccupied in what they are doing. They are curious. They take risks. They are flexible in their opinions. They are intellectually self-confident.

Socially Disadvantaged Children

Most teachers encounter a group of children in their classrooms who appear lifeless, incurious, and deceptively unintelligent. They show lack of interest, involvement, and motivation for academic success. They show general academic underachievement. The cumulative deficiencies in learning ultimately lead to their wastage and stagnation. These children are socially, economically, and educationally disadvantaged. School readiness programme in pre-school centers, enriched experiences, and remedial instruction are very useful for them.

Delinquent Children

In school teachers come across some children who violate school norms. They are defiant of social standards. They are involved in anti-social activities or criminal activities which are punishable under law. If such children are in the age-group of 12 to 18, if their anti-social activities are serious in nature and occur very frequently they are considered as delinquents.

2

Educational Programmes for Children with Special Needs —A Historical Perspective

"There have always been special needs children, but there have not always been educational programmes to meet their needs." It is, therefore, pertinent to give some thoughts to the historical perspectives of educational programmes for special needs children.

Remedial education, compensatory education, special education, special classes, the whole school approach, integration—these and many more have had their brief heyday in the field and have, in due course, disappeared into history just as the term 'integration' is now being overtaken by the term 'inclusion.'

Given this unstable past, one would imagine that some sort of historical perspective would be an integral part of our study. "In reality, however, we are not very good at remembering our past, much less at connecting it with our present" (Dyson, 2001). The history of educational programmes for children with special needs presents both an optimistic and a pessimistic picture.

The optimistic picture indicates that the practice and policy in special needs education have improved over time; that the attitude of society towards the less fortunate children has changed over the centuries, though much slowly; and that in past things were done less well than they are now, or, indeed, entirely the wrong things were done.

The pessimistic picture indicates how some groups of influential people, though small in number, conspired to subvert any progress towards more liberal practices; how the interests of these less fortunate children were damaged by those who claimed to serve them; and how the conservative forces worked to maintain the status quo. Thus the pessimistic view has little to offer beyond a sorry tale of thwarted initiatives and shattered ideals. It is, therefore, pertinent to study how change has taken place—from superstitions to segregation, and later to integration, and what the direction of change is taking place at present.

SUPERSTITION

In the earliest primitive societies, particularly in Egypt, Greek and Rome, disabled babies were killed because they were considered to be imperfect. The guiding principle was "Nothing imperfect should be brought up." During Middle Ages, the rise of deep religious convictions throughout the world produced some humanitarian care for the retarded, mentally ill, and physically handicapped. The threat to survival of disabled children decreased, but the mentally ill were considered to be possessed by evil spirits or demons. Mental and physical abnormalities were considered to be the result of anger of God, or the divine punishment for a sin. The primary treatment consisted of driving the spirit from the possessed by pleasing God through prayer and rituals. Throughout history there have been people who viewed mental illness as a disease, and not the result of possession by demons. However, their voices were rarely heard by the majority.

In most parts of India, the idea that a disabled child is the result of the anger of God, or ancestors, or the embodiment of a sin was widely prevalent. Even at present, parents of disabled children feel guilty and sometimes take the blame for the impairment on themselves. Disabled children are considered to be useless and a burden for the family. In some cases, disabled infants are left at the gates of temple or churches, abandoned in institutions or left to live helplessly in the corner of a room. The fate of disabled girls is still worse.

SEGREGATION

Benjamin Rush, a physician in the late 1700s, was one of the first Americans to introduce the idea of educating persons with disabilities J.M.S Itard, a French physician was the originator of instructional devices, the inventor of behaviour modification techniques, the first speech therapist, creator of oral education of the deaf, the father of special education for the mentally retarded and the physically handicapped. His work with Victor, a wild boy of 11 or 12, established the idea that the retarded could learn and improve. In 1817, Thomas Gallaudet established the first special school for the education of the deaf at Hartford. In 1829, the New England Asylum for the education of the blind was founded in Watertown, Massachusetts. E. Seguin established the first special school for the feeble minded in Paris. In 1846, he published his classic textbook, *Idiocy and Its Treatment by the Physiological Method*. The first Experimental School for Teaching and Training Idiotic Children was founded in 1846 in Barre, Massachusetts.

As per the *Encyclopaedia of Special Education*, the establishment of special education began in 1832 with the first school for the deaf in Kentucky. The first College for the Deaf (Gallaudet College) was started in 1857 in Colombia. In 1896, Rhode Island began education classes for individuals with mental retardation. The first remedial centers were set up in England in the late 1940s (Golby and Gulliver, 1985).

At the conclusion of the American War of Independence, a number of philanthrophic organizations played a leading role in the establishment of training institutions for people with disabilities. Some leaders of special education at the time, such as Samuel Gridley Howe, made remarkable efforts for the education of blind and deaf children. Howe's phenomenal success with one of his pupils—Laura Bridgmen, a deaf-dumb-blind, again established the fact that pupils with disabilities could be educated. This trend towards segregated education reached its high point during the 20th century.

Segregated institutions for individuals with disabilities continued to grow in numbers and size during the late 19th century until the 1950s. Concurrently, another trend was developing—the creation of public "common schools" where most children were educated. However, various groups of children were excluded from the mainstream of public schools. For example, students with visible and significant disabilities continued, for the most part, to be segregated. Residential institutions and special schools remained the norm for educating students who were blind or deaf or had physical disabilities. Students with significant developmental disabilities were generally denied educational services of any types. "Almost all children who were wheel-chair-bound, not toilet-trained, or considered ineducable were excluded because of problems that schooling would entail" (Sigmon, 1983).

Along with establishment of special schools, special classes in public schools were also expanded in some cases for education of children with disabilities. "Special classes came about not for humanitarian reasons, but because such children were unwanted in the regular classroom" (Chaves, 1977). Another notable feature is that special educators were in a regular school, but in many ways were not part of it. General and special education developed on parallel rather than converging lines. But during the 1950s and 1960s, the use of special classes in public schools was the preferred educational delivery system for most students with disabilities. It was during this period that public attitude about the place of individuals with disabilities in schools and in the community began to change.

In India, segregated education of children with disabilities began with the establishment of the first special schools in Amritsar in 1887 by Anne Sharp, a missionary manager (Mani, 1988; Mukherjee, 1986; Pandey and Advani, 1997). However, Miles (1997) also reports that the first special school for mentally retarded and physically handicapped children began in India at Kurseong in 1918. The education of children with disabilities continued to be provided in segregated settings following India's independence in 1947. Of course, various NGOs assumed increasing responsibilities for the education of children with different types of disabilities. There were more than 1200 special schools by 1997 (Pandey & Advani, 1997). The exact figure of special schools for children with different types of disabilities at present is not available.

THE MOVEMENT TOWARDS INTEGRATION

During 1950s and 1960s parents' organizations in USA initiated advocacy actions for education of their children with disabilities. A group of special education leaders, such as Blatt, Dunn, Cruickshank, Hobbs, Lilly, and Wolfensberger began advocating for the rights of students with disabilities to learn in more normalized school environment with their peers. During this period, a large number of special educators were exploring the possibilities of integrating children with disabilities into the regular classrooms. For example, Klaus Wedell was encouraging hearing-impaired children from a segregated unit in Bristol, England to join in mainstream classroom activities. Similarly, Peter Mittler was working to integrate children with autistic spectrum disorders from a hospital setting into mainstream primary schools in England in the early 1960s. These two examples indicate that special educators were thinking towards "integration", before the term was coined. For the first time, and on a fairly wide basis, the restrictions imposed by segregated institutions, special schools, and special classes were presented as problematic. The wheel of change had been set in motion.

In the early part of 1970s, various court decisions in USA established the right of all children labeled as mentally retarded to free and appropriate education. Pressure by parents, courts and legislators resulted in Education for All Handicapped Children Act of 1975 (PL. 94-142) which was enacted in 1978. This law, reauthorized as the Individuals With Disabilities Education of 1990 (PL. 101-407) extended the right to a free public education to all children, regardless of disability, in the least restrictive environment possible. The term 'integration' was thus formally introduced in 1978 (Peter Clough, 2000).

By the late 1970s and early 1980s, many disabled students began to be integrated into the regular classroom on at least a part time basis. By the 1980s, attempts to educate children with disabilities in the regular classroom on a full time basis were intensified. Integrated education for disabled children was the favoured practice in all countries up to 1994 World Conference on Special Education Needs at Salamanca, Spain.

A number of international and national initiatives have contributed significantly to the movement towards integrated education in India.

The Indian Education Commission (1964-66) was the first statutory body to suggest that "education of handicapped children has to be organized not merely on humanitarian grounds but also on grounds of reality." The Commission also emphasized that the education of handicapped children should be an "inseparable part of the general education system." In order to provide adequate services to handicapped children, the Commission recommended for adoption of two approaches, namely, special education and integrated education.

Integration of children with disabilities into the regular classroom could draw the attention of State Governments after the Ministry of Welfare, Government of India initiated the Scheme of Integrated Education for Disabled Children (IEDC) in 1974. The Centrally Sponsored Scheme of IEDC was revised in 1981 and later in 1992 allowing 100 per cent assistance to State Governments for implementing the scheme. Moreover, non-government organizations (NGOs) are now being involved in providing education to disabled children in the regular classroom. As per the report (Azad, 1996), the scheme is now being implemented in 24 States and Union Territories serving 44,000 students in more than 11,000 schools.

The United Nations declared 1981 as the International Year of Disabled Persons. "Full Participation with Equality" was the underlying theme of this programme. India's response to the UN's declaration was the development of a National Plan of Action to provide comprehensive services including integrated education for persons with disabilities.

In 1986, the National Policy on Education (NPE) was formulated which was revised in 1992. The NPE (1986/1992) emphasized that "Wherever feasible, education of children with locomotor handicap and other mild handicaps will be common with that of others." The NPE (1986/1992) also states that those children whose needs cannot be met in regular schools are to be enrolled in special schools. As soon as the disabled children enrolled in special schools acquire reasonable levels of daily living skills, communication skills and basic academic skills they will be integrated into the regular schools. As per the NPE (1986/1992), "The objective should be to integrate the physically and mentally handicapped with the general community, to prepare them for normal growth and to enable them to face life with courage and confidence."

In 1987, the Project Integrated Education for the Disabled (PIED) was implemented by the Ministry of Human Resource Development, Government of India on a composite area approach to strengthen the Scheme of IEDC. About 13,000 children with disabilities in 8 states and 2 urban slums were benefited in the project. Over 9,000 teachers received training to work with disabled children in integrated setting (Azad, 1996).

Rule 6 of the UN Standard Rules for Persons with Disabilities (1992) states : "States should recognize the principle of equal primary, secondary and tertiary educational opportunities for children, youth and adults with disabilities in integrated settings. They should ensure that the education of persons with disabilities is an integral part of the education system. General education authorities are responsible for the education of persons with disabilities in integrated settings. Education of persons with disabilities should form an integral part of national educational planning, curriculum development and school organizations" (Quoted by Rao, 2003). India was a signatory to the UN Standard Rules for Persons with Disabilities.

In 1992, the Economic and Social Commission for Asia and the Pacific (ESCAP), at its 48th session held in Beijing declared 1993-2002 as the Asian and Pacific Decade for

Disabled Persons. India attended the ESCAP Committee meeting and pledged to implement the recommendations on full participation and equality of people with disabilities in the fields of rehabilitation, education and employment including promotion of integration of children and adults with disabilities in formal and non-formal educational programmes.

The District Primary Education Programme (DPEP), a major internationally assisted programme was launched in the country to reform and renew the primary education system of the country. It was implemented in selected districts in a phased manner. One significant feature of DPEP is its emphasis on integrated education for the disabled.

The remaining districts which were not covered under DPEP, are being covered under Sarva Shiksha Abhiyan (SSA) which represents the latest and the all subsuming initiative for universal elementary education in the country. The SSA vision is to provide useful and relevant elementary education of satisfactory quality for all by 2010, bridging all social and gender gaps with the active participation of the community in the school affairs. The goals of SSA are:

- All children shall be in school, Education Guarantee Centre, Alternate School, Back to School Camp.
- All children shall complete five years of schooling by 2007.
- All children shall complete eight years elementary education by 2010.
- Focus on elementary education of satisfactory quality with emphasis on education for life.
- Bridging all gender and social gaps by 2010.

Although the Government of India had made several attempts to integrate disabled into the regular classrooms, it lacked in firm commitment to promote integration. The Persons With Disability Act (PWD Act) 1995, has made integration of students with disability a legal responsibility of the Government. The PWD Act (1995) states, among other things:

The appropriate Government and the local authorities shall ensure that every child with a disability has access to free education in an appropriate environment till he attains the age of 18 years (Article 26a); endeavor to promote the integration of students with disabilities in the normal schools (Article 26b).

In spite of all these polities and acts integrated education could not succeed in terms of:

- Enrolment of children with disabilities.
- Perception of teaches about the educability of these children.
- Acceptance and respect by teachers and peers.
- Collaboration of teachers for providing quality education to such children.
- Leadership of head teachers.
- Involvement of parents.
- Community support, etc. (Dash, 2001).

The trend, at present, is directed towards inclusive education.

Inclusive Education

3

INCLUSION—A WORLDWIDE MOVEMENT

Historically we have had two educational systems—one for children with disabilities (education in special schools) and one for everyone else (education in regular classroom). The movement towards integration of children with disabilities into the regular classrooms started in the second half of the twentieth century. The trend at present is to create one education system that values all children—to devise a classroom that welcomes all children irrespective of disability, community background, sexuality, ethnic background, etc.

Julka (2001) has traced the path of inclusion figuratively in the following way:

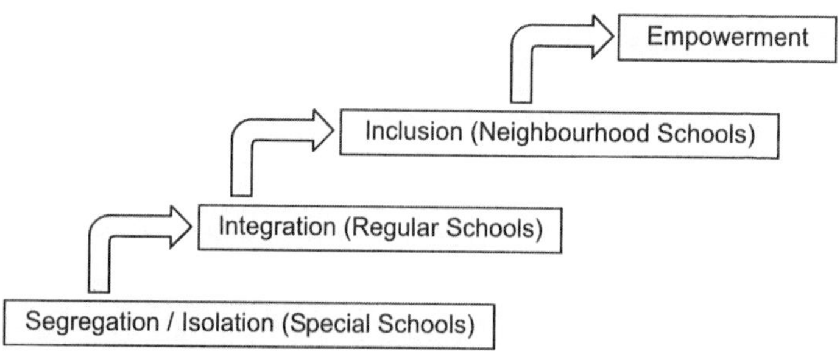

As the figure indicates the policy for the provision of facilities for children with special needs has progressed from segregation in special schools to inclusion in the neighbourhood schools which aims at empowerment of all children.

Internationally, the drive towards inclusion of children with special needs into the mainstream of regular schools is fuelled by a number of initiatives and treaties including the

UN Convention on the Rights of the Child (1987), the UN Standard Rules on the Equalization of Opportunities for Persons with Disabilities (1993), Jomtien World Declaration on Education for All (1990) and the World Conference on Special Needs Education (1994).

The Word Declaration on Education for All. Jomtien, Thailand, which was reaffirmed in the Dakar Framework for Action (2000), gives the message:

> In order to attract and retain children from marginalized and excluded groups, education systems should respond flexibly. Education systems must be inclusive, actively seeking out children who are not enrolled, and responding flexibly to the circumstances and needs of all learners......

In 1994, representatives of 92 governments and 25 international organizations formed the World Conference on Special Needs Education in Salamanca, Spain. They agreed a new dynamic statement on the education of all disabled children, which called for 'inclusion to be the norm'. Paragraph 2 is the key statement of belief and comprises five clauses.

The first clause states a view on children's rights: every child has a fundamental right to education, and must be given the opportunity to achieve and maintain an acceptable level of learning.

The second clause asserts each child's uniqueness; every child has uniqueness; every child has unique characteristics, interests, abilities and learning needs.

The third clause states a belief about how the education system should operate as a consequence of this premise; education systems should be designed and educational programmes should be implemented to take into account the wide diversity of these characteristics and needs.

The fourth clause develops this line, stating requirements; those with special educational needs must have access to regular schools, which should accommodate them within a child-centred pedagogy capable of meeting these needs.

Finally, clause five provides a rationale for regular schools: regular schools with this inclusive orientation are the most effective means of combating discriminatory attitude, creating welcoming communities, building an inclusive society, and achieving education for all; moreover, they provide an effective education for the majority of children and improve the efficiency and ultimately the cost-effectiveness of the entire education system.

The World Conference went on to call upon all governments to:

(a) Give the highest policy and budgetary priority to improve education services so that all children could be included regardless of differences or difficulties.

(b) Adopt as a matter of law or policy the principle of inclusive education and enrol all children in regular schools unless there were compelling reasons for doing otherwise.

(c) Develop demonstration projects and encourage exchange with countries with inclusive schools.

(d) Ensure that organizations of disabled people along with parents and community bodies are involved in planning and decision-making.

(e) Put greater efforts into pre-school strategies as well as vocational aspects of inclusive education.

(f) Ensure that both initial and in-service training address the provision of inclusive education.

The statement calls on the international community to endorse the approach of inclusive schooling and to support the development of special needs education as an integral part of all education programmes. In particular, it calls on UNESCO, UNICEF, UNDP and the World Bank for this endorsement.

Inclusive education which has emerged as a reform in the education of children with special needs gained momentum since 1994 World Conference on Special Needs Education. It is significant that some countries have made significant advances towards promoting inclusive education in their legislation. Examples include: Canada, Cyprus, Denmark, Iceland, India, Luxembourg, Malta, the Netherlands, Norway,

South Africa, Spain, Sweden, Uganda, the United Kingdom, Australia and the United States. At the same time inclusion has been the subject of heated debate in professional journals, training programmes for teacher educators and among special education leaders. What does inclusion imply? What is inclusive education? What does an inclusive classroom look like? How is the inclusive approach different from the traditional approach? These are some of the fundamental questions which need to be attended in any study on inclusive education.

THE CONCEPT OF INCLUSION/INCLUSIVE EDUCATION/ INCLUSIVE SCHOOL

In looking up a dictionary definition of the term 'inclusion' we are directed to the verbal form, 'to include' which is defined as: 'to have as a part; contain in addition to other parts or to put in with something or someone else; take in or consider as part of a group' (*Longman's English Dictionary*).

In education, 'inclusion' refers to the placement and education of children with disabilities in regular education classrooms with children of the same age who do not have disabilities. The underlying premise of inclusion is that all children can learn and belong to the mainstream of school and community life. Inclusion is a basic value that extends to all children. Inclusion gives a message:

Everyone belongs to the school.
Everyone is welcome to the school.

In the words of Loreman and Deppeler (2001) "Inclusion means full inclusion of children with diverse abilities (that is both giftedness and disability) in all aspects of schooling that other children are able to access and enjoy. It involves 'regular' schools and classrooms genuinely adapting and changing to meet the needs of all children as well as celebrating and valuing differences."

This definition of inclusion does not imply that children with diverse abilities will not receive specialized assistance or teaching outside of the classroom when required, but rather that this is just one of many options that are available to, and in fact required of, all children.

The goal of inclusion is to ensure that all children, regardless of any individual differences they may have, are fully included in the mainstream of life. But we do not know the time frame when all children will be fully included in the mainstream of school and community.

Inclusion is the provision of services to students with special needs in the neighbourhood schools with necessary support services and supplementary aids for both children and teachers. It means meeting the needs of all children with and without disabilities for a free and quality public education in the least restrictive and most effective environment of the neighbourhood schools.

Inclusion does not mean 'dumping' children with special needs into the regular classroom. We have to accept their diversity, respect their individuality, create opportunities for their participation in all activities of the school, and provide support to both children and teachers so that children can realize their full potential and teachers will be able to improve their performances. Thomas (1997) has defined inclusion as the "acceptance of all pupils in the mainstream system, taught with a common framework, and identified as the responsibility of all teachers."

> Inclusion is a process (rather than a specific ideology or set of practices). It is not merely about providing access into mainstream school for pupils who have previously been excluded. It is not about closing down an unacceptable system of segregated provision and dumping these pupils in an unchanged mainstream system. Existing school systems—in terms of physical factors, curriculum aspects, teaching expectations and styles, leadership roles—will have to change. This is because inclusive education is about the participation of all children and young people and the removal of all forms of exclusionary practices (Bartons, 1998).

> Inclusion is a term which can be defined as an attitude or a commitment of appreciating diversities and accepting that

all children can be educated in a common school to their maximum potential. It requires increasing the capacity of regular schools so that they can respond creatively to greater diversities. It also involves building the capacities of teachers to deal with diverse population of students and to acquire pedagogical competencies that facilitate the learning of all students in their classroom (Julka, 2001).

Booth (1999) emphasizes three criteria for inclusive education system such as, increasing the participation, reducing exclusion and giving equality when he says — "I define inclusive education as the process of increasing the participation of learners within, and reducing their exclusion from the cultures, curricula and communities of neighbourhood centres of learning...

...It is about giving learners an equality of regard irrespective of their background, gender, ethnicity, sexuality, disability and attainment."

Lindsay (2003) has very rightly stated: "It (inclusive education) is championed as a means to remove barriers, improve outcomes, and remove discrimination. Inclusion is, however, a complex and contested concept and its manifestations in practice are many and various."

What does an inclusive school look like? "A school that promotes inclusive education is called an inclusive school. An inclusive school is a place where everyone belongs, is accepted, supports and is supported by his or her peers and other members of the school community in the course of having his or her educational needs met" (Stainback, Stainback & Forest, 1989). Inclusive schooling is the process of operating a classroom or school as a supportive community where the needs of all members are met and people support and accept responsibility for each other.

According to Thomas, Walker & Webb (1998), "an inclusive school contains the following elements:

It is *community based*: an inclusive school reflects the community as a whole. Membership of the school community is open, positive and diverse; it is not selective, exclusive or rejecting; it is *barrier-free*; an inclusive school is accessible to all who become members — physically in terms of the buildings and grounds, and educationally in terms of curricula support systems and methods of communication; it promotes *collaboration*; an inclusive school works with, rather than competitively against, other schools; it promotes *equality*, an inclusive school is a democracy."

Inclusive classrooms look different all the time because the environment is created by whatever interactions the teacher and students have as a group or as individuals in the group. It is a classroom where a lot of students do different things with peers and teachers helping them. It is a classroom where students move from one environment to another. It is also a classroom where everybody is smiling, the students are actively engaged, and the teacher is delighted to be there. It is a classroom where teachers come with lot of preparation, clear vision and strong commitments. But it is difficult to get such ideal classrooms always. But "Inclusion without resources, without commitment, without a vision statement, without restructuring, and without staff development won't work." Mara Sapon-Shevlin (2003) (www.uni.edu/coe/inclusion/strategies/inclusiveclassroom.html).

WHAT IS NOT INCLUSION?

We sometimes find that educators are misinformed and confused about inclusion. Part of the confusion strikes at the heart of the matter and arises from the meaning of the term itself. Inclusion cannot exist in environments where some children are educated separately or substantively different to their peers. It is perhaps easier to provide examples of what is not inclusion:

(i) Inclusion does not mean dumping children with special needs into the regular classrooms as is noticed in most schools of our country under SSA.

(ii) Educating children in special, mostly segregated environments in regular schools is not inclusion.

(iii) Educating children part-time in special schools and part-time in regular schools is not inclusion.

(iv) Educating children in regular schools, but requiring them to follow substantially different courses of study in terms of content and learning environment to their peers is also not inclusion (unless all children in a class follow individual programmes).

TRADITIONAL APPROACH AND INCLUSIVE APPROACH

Until recently children with special needs were educated with traditional approach. The trend, at present, is to educate all children with inclusive approach. How is the new inclusive approach different from the old traditional approach?

Johnson (1995) answers the question by making a distinction between traditional approach and inclusive approach. According to him: the inclusive approach calls for certain reforms in school practices as is evident from Table 3.1.

Table 3.1: Distinction Between Traditional Approach and Inclusive Approach

Traditional Approach	*Inclusive Approach*
Education for some	Education for all
Static/Rigid	Flexible
Collective Teaching	Individualized Teaching
Learning in Segregated settings	Learning in Integrated settings
Emphasis on Teaching	Emphasis on Learning
Subject-centred	Child-centred
Diagnostic/Prescriptive	Holistic
Opportunities Limited by exclusion	Equalization of opportunities for all
Disability View	Curricular View
Labels Children	Planning is made on Ability
Disability wise	Label-Free

Source: Johnson, T., *Inclusive Education*, UNDP, Geneva, 1995.

INTEGRATED EDUCATION AND INCLUSIVE EDUCATION

Any discussion on the concept of inclusion needs to make a clear distinction between 'inclusion' and 'integration' since the later term has been, and continues to be, extensively used, sometimes synonymously with inclusion. Ware (1995), for example, suggests that "inclusive education describes the restructuring of special education to permit all or most students to be integrated in mainstream classes through reorganization and instructional innovations (e.g., cooperative learning, collaborative consultation and team teaching)." However, use of the term 'integrated' is somewhat confusing here. But the later part of her statement provides the key elements to differentiate between inclusion and integration.

Integration involves coming from the outside. Integration programmes aim to involve children with diverse abilities into the existing classes and structures within a school. They endeavour to 'normalise,' to help a child fit into the pre-existing model of schooling. Inclusion assumes that all children are a part of the regular school system from the very beginning of school. The need, therefore, for children to adapt to a school setting is not an issue as they are already a part of that system. One goal of inclusion is for every school to be ready in advance to accept children with diverse abilities. This may involve not only a change in the way our schools are structured and work, but also a change in the attitudes of regular education teachers who view their job as to educate non-disabled children. Most schools advocate the use of a child-centred approach to education which implies that all teachers should be willing to meet the needs of all children (Loreman, 1999).

Inclusive education usually involves focusing on an individual pupil or small groups of pupils for whom the curriculum is adapted, different work is devised or support is provided. Integration does not necessarily alter in any way the organisation and provision of curriculum. Thus in integrated education the child is expected to fit into the existing curriculum, but in inclusive education the curriculum is adapted to fit to the needs of every child. "Inclusion, therefore, is conceptualized not as how to assimilate individual pupils with SEN into existing forms of schooling, but, instead, as how schools can be restructured in order to respond positively to all pupils as individuals."

"Inclusion values diversity, not assimilation" (Ballard, 1995)

In integrated education, support, if any, comes from the resource teacher and is meant for specific categories of children who are defined as having special needs. In inclusive education support comes from the whole school community and can be of benefit to many pupils. Udvari-solner & Thousand (1995) suggest: "Inclusive education is seen as a process of operating a classroom or school as a supportive community. Thus, it is different from integration or mainstreaming which focuses upon how to help a particular category of students to fit into mainstream."

Inclusion is not a new label for mainstreaming or integration as some people tend to think. It is related to but different from the movement to integrate or mainstream students with disabilities into the regular neighbourhood schools. Mainstreaming was an educational philosophy and practice, which assumed the existence of two separate systems—regular education and special education. Inclusive education assumes the existence of only one education system for all children. Of course, this does not mean closing down all special schools. Rather, special schools can function as resource centres for inclusive schools.

> An inclusive school and the process of inclusive schooling is the ultimate goal of integration and mainstreaming. Once inclusive schooling is achieved integration and mainstreaming will no longer be necessary since there will no longer be anyone left out to be integrated or mainstreamed into regular educational settings. (Stainback and Stainback, 1990).

In the existing system of integration, students with disabilities are educated in physical proximity to their age-peers, but significant attention is not paid to qualitative features of this arrangement. In inclusive settings, the focus is on how to develop supportive classrooms and schools that fit, nurture and support the educational and social needs of every student in attendance. Integrated education focuses on the deficiencies of the child. Inclusive education focuses on the quality of schooling.

The IDDC seminar on inclusive education, 1998, gave the following diagrams to explain the differences between integrated education and inclusive education(www.eenet.org.uk/documents/reports/agra/digram/html).

INTEGRATED EDUCATION

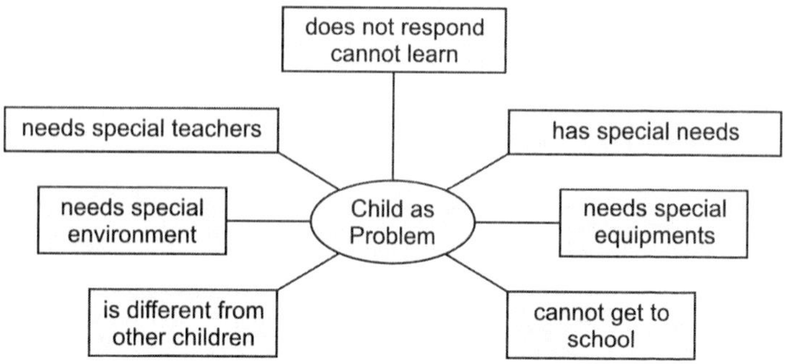

INCLUSIVE EDUCATION

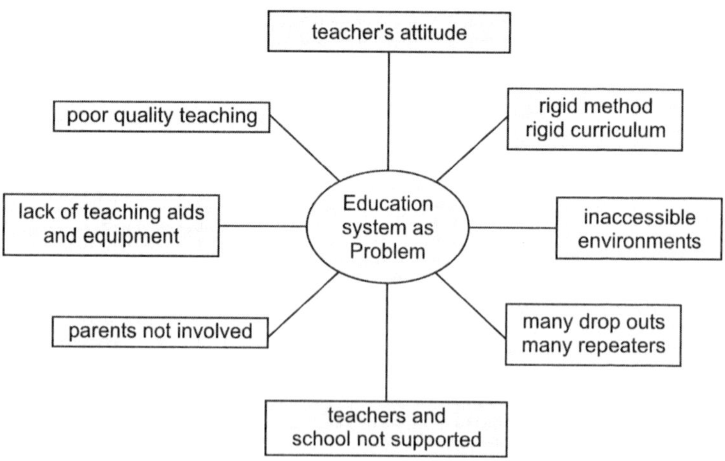

Justification of Inclusive Education

4

Why should inclusive education be promoted? Why does it matter? What are the reasons for justifying inclusive education for children with disabilities? Inclusive education for children with disabilities can be justified from educational perspectives, sociological point of view, economic point of view, humanitarian point of view, democratic point of view and legal perspectives. Inclusive education can also be justified in terms of its benefits for children with disability and those without disability including gifted children.

EDUCATIONAL PERSPECTIVES

Inclusive schooling is the practice of including everyone—irrespective of talent, disability, socio-economic background, or cultural origin—in supportive mainstream school and classrooms where the needs of all students are met. By educating all children together, children with disabilities have the opportunity to prepare for life in the community, teachers improve their professional skills, and society makes the conscious decision to operate according to the social value of equality. The justification of inclusive education can be discussed in terms of benefit to students, teachers and society.

In the words of Vandercook, Fleetham, Sinclair, and Tetlie (1988), in inclusive classrooms all children are enriched by having the opportunity to learn from one another, grow to care for one another, and gain the attitudes, skills and values necessary for our communities. When proper arrangements are present, inclusion works for all students with and without disabilities in terms of mutually held positive attitudes, gains in academic and social skills, and preparation for living in the community. With appropriate guidance and direction from adults inclusion helps to develop friendship and positive peer interaction. Students learn to be sensitive to understand, respect and grow comfortable with individual differences and similarities among their peers.

Apart from positive attitudes, researches have repeatedly shown the tremendous benefits that children gain from socialization with their peers during the school years. Children learn many academic skills as well as daily life, communication, and social skills (Cullinan, Sabornie, and Crossland 1992) through sustained interactions with their peers.

For cognitive development to proceed, environmental demands must gradually increase. Including handicapped and non-handicapped children in the classrooms has the potential to create an appropriately demanding environment for the handicapped children—an environment that will facilitate continued development. Too often, segregated schools have taken the path of making too few demands on their pupils. It is likely that once handicapped and non-handicapped children are grouped together, teachers and parents may develop more realistic expectations about what the handicapped children should be attempting to do. The non-handicapped peers will play a very important role in expecting and encouraging behaviour. Inclusive classrooms create the opportunity for handicapped children to imitate the behaviour of non-handicapped models. When these positive effects are contrasted with the negative effects of exclusion, the benefits of inclusive schools become even more pronounced. Academically, socially and occupationally segregated placements are damaging to students. Wehman (1990) conducted a series of studies and concluded that "segregated classes do not lead to independence and competence, but instead foster an unrealistic sense of insulation."

Inclusive education has also benefits to teachers. The fate of schools in our evolving society is changing and teachers must acquire new skills in working with students who are academically and socially disadvantaged. In this transformation of the teaching profession, teachers have the opportunity to develop their professional skills in an atmosphere of collegiality, collaboration, and peer support. In inclusive education, teachers have the opportunity to plan and conduct the business of education as part of a team. Many teachers feel alienated in school because the ethic of teaching by one's self provides few or no chances for supportive peer interaction. Inclusive schools allow collaboration and consultation among teachers and this provides psychological support to them. Peer collaboration and consultation help teachers to improve their professional capabilities. Inclusive schooling provides opportunity to teachers to participate in decision-making and shaping the daily life of the school. "Teachers are (therefore) empowered by elevating their status, keeping themselves informed of changes occurring in their fields and ensuring that they participate in decision-making" (Sindelar, Griffin, Smith and Watanabe, 1992).

By far the most important reason for inclusive schooling is the social value of equality. We have to teach students by example that despite differences, we all have equal rights. In contrast to the past experiences of segregation, inclusion reinforces the practice of the idea that differences are accepted and respected. Because our society is in a critical phase of evolving from industrial to informational and from national to international, it is important that we avoid the mistakes of the past. We need schools that promote wider social acceptance, peace, and cooperation.

SOCIOLOGICAL POINT OF VIEW

According to Stainback and Stainback (1990), "If a society supports integration of all individuals, then segregated schools and classrooms have no place in that society. There is no defensible rationale, excuse, nor scientific research that can be conducted that will in the final analysis justify segregation."

In our society we have people from different cultural, religious and ethnic background. Our people must accept, respect and appreciate each other's background. Thus our children must be educated accordingly right from their primary education level. For this, we need schools that promote wider social acceptance, peace and cooperation. Social acceptance in the work place and the community at large is born out of opportunities for people with disabilities to function, perform normalized tasks, and interact with their peers in school. Equally important is for their peers to learn how to interact with them (Westwood, 1998). Inclusive schools promote acceptance, respect and support among children with and without disabilities. When schools exclude some students, prejudice is entrenched in the consciousness of many students when they become adults, with the result of increased social conflict and dehumanizing competition.

Inclusive education makes good social sense. Segregation teaches children to be fearful, ignorant and breeds prejudice. All children need an education that will help them develop relationships and prepare them for life in the mainstream. Only inclusion has the potential to reduce fear and to build friendship, respect and understanding (*CSIE Report*, 2002).

In the opening address to the Victorian Federation of State School Parent's Club Seminar on Integration of Children with Disabilities into local schools (November, 1981), Dr. Graham Clunies – Ross, the then Head of the Department of Educational Psychology at Melbourne State College stated "Societal attitudes towards the child with disability may be altered positively through integration." What Graham stated in 1981 about integration holds true for inclusive education today. "Inclusion of children with disabilities in regular classes and social and recreational activities can result in more positive ratings of disabled children by non-disabled children. For non-handicapped children to gain knowledge about, understanding of, tolerance for, and to be able to learn to accept handicapped children, it is essential that handicapped and non-handicapped children be involved in the same developmentally formative setting."

ECONOMIC PERSPECTIVES

In a country like India inclusive education for children with disabilities is justified from economic perspectives. This is evident from the following facts:

There are an estimated 600 million persons with one form of disability or the other all over the world and 10 per cent of this number is estimated to be in India. That means we have 60 million persons with disability (Disability, April 2003). 97 per cent of disabled children in developing countries are without any form of rehabilitation. 98 per cent of disabled children are without any education (Disability, 2003). A recent article by Kenneth Eklindh of UNESCO states: More than 90 per cent of disabled children in developing countries are not in school (Education Today, Oct-Nov. 2003).

According to Child Relief and You (CRY), 3 per cent of India's children are estimated to be mentally challenged. Of these 15 million children are below the age of 10 years. 10 million are boys and 5 million are girls. 20 per cent of disabled children are in the urban areas and 80 per cent of disabled children are in the rural areas. Of course there are inter and intra state variations. It is also a fact that most of the children with disabilities belong to the economically lower brackets.

The estimated figures about disabled children in our country are really horrifying. We cannot ignore this segment of our population while planning for education, development and employment. The Government of India in the Ministry of Human Resource Development has launched Sarva Sikhsa Abhiyan which also includes children with disabilities. The flagship programme, "Sarva Shiksha Abhiyan" launched in 2000 aims at completion of five years of primary education to all children by 2007, completion of eight years of education to all children by 2010, provision of elementary quality education by 2010 and universal retention by 2010 (Address by the former Union Minister for HRD, Dr. M.M. Joshi in the Commonwealth Education Ministers' Conference at Edinburgh on October 29, 2003). The problem faced at present is how to provide education to such a vast population of disabled children. There are two alternatives: education in special schools and education in regular schools in the neighbourhood.

According to the Sixth All India Educational Survey report, of the 6461 towns and cities, only 334 or 5.1 per cent towns and cities have the facility of special schools catering to the needs of children with severe disabilities. In these towns, a total of 630 schools, out of 928 schools on record, are actually functioning. The number of special schools in towns and cities is not adequate enough to provide education to children with disabilities living in urban areas.

The situation in the villages is even more dismal. Of the total 586,465 villages in our country, a mere 241 villages have facilities of special schools catering to all types of disabilities. Out of 296 special schools on record 272 schools are actually functioning in rural areas. The number of special schools in rural areas is too small to meet the needs of disabled children living in rural areas who constitute nearly 80 per cent of the disabled children. What is the way out? Should additional special schools be set up to cater to the needs of vast number of disabled children? Establishment of additional special schools is expensive and a country like India cannot afford to spend so much of money to adequately serve all children.

A cost analysis by WHO (1997) indicates that it is more expensive to set up separate institutions that cater to special segments of the populations than it is to invest in their integration. Building an institution costs in terms of sustainability and reaches out to a comparative handful of disabled people, who may remain economically passive recipients throughout their lives. Traditionally most of the money spent on disability services either goes into buildings or into paying the salaries of professionals and administrators rather than into local, rights-based initiatives. The solution to this expenditure should not be to cut costs but to redirect the funding to initiatives that support disabled peoples' rights, lead to their integration in society and thereby contribute to society-enabling in the process the activation of positive attitudes. The Salamanca Statement also affirms inclusive education as cost-effective. In short, inclusive education is cost-effective in view of the following considerations.

Establishment of additional special schools is expensive in terms of building cost, salaries of teachers, provision of aids and equipment, transportation etc. as compared to including children with disabilities in their neighbourhood schools where education and care of such children become the responsibility of each and every teacher.

In view of the financial constraints of State Governments, it is not feasible at present or in near future to set-up new special schools in each village/town to cater to the needs of children with disabilities.

Education in special schools managed by NGO and voluntary organizations is considered to be expensive, in practice, though not necessarily in pen and paper.

Most parents of disabled children are not able to meet the expenses of educating their children in special schools. So they are bound to keep their children in their homes depriving them of their basic right. When disabled children are kept in homes, parents cannot leave them alone and go out for work. This adds additional burden to the family income. If such children are sent to neighbourhood schools parents need not spend much on their education. They can go out for work. Children with disabilities who receive education become self-supporting members of the family in future, and not a burden for parents.

HUMANITARIAN POINT OF VIEW

The humanitarian point of view is based on the principle of normalization. This states that the child with disability should have the same range of opportunities, experiences and conditions of everyday life that are typically available to non-disabled children in the community and that appropriate development and educational programmes should be provided to enable the disabled child to share in, contribute to and benefit maximally from everyday life. It seems that the only way we can be sure that disabled children will have the same range of educational opportunities and experiences as non-disabled children is to have their education provided for in the same setting. As in the past, it is abundantly clear that many disabled children today still have their development retarded because they are segregated into schools and classes which offer a restricted range of educational opportunities and experiences. Lack of self-confidence, lack of motivation and lack of positive expectations for achievements are all products of segregated learning environment (Stainback, Stainback and Forest, 1989). Segregation generates a feeling of inferiority as to children's status in the community that may affect their hearts and minds. This sense of inferiority affects the motivation of a child to learn and retards his educational and mental development.

Every child with and without disability has enormous potential for growth. A disabled child has also potential to be extremely successful in independent community living and career of his choice. He can find jobs for himself and live as self supporting, socially competent member of society. The ability of the child with disability to succeed in the community is directly related to the amount of training and support that he receives while he is in school. Inclusive school is the appropriate setting to help these children realize their full potential.

The Framework for Action (Salamanca Statement) says: "Inclusion and participation are essential to human dignity and to the enjoyment and exercise of human rights." In the field of education, this is reflected in bringing about a genuine equalization of opportunity. Human differences are normal and that instruction must be adapted to the needs of the child, rather than the child fitted to the process. The fundamental principle of the inclusive school is that all children should learn together, where possible, and that regular schools must recognize and respond to the diverse needs of their students.

DEMOCRATIC POINT OF VIEW

One important reason for including all children in the mainstream is that it is the fair, ethical, and equitable measure to do. Inclusive education promotes the value of equality. But separate is not equal. Thus all students should be a part of the educational and community mainstream. It is discriminatory that some students such as those labeled disabled must earn the right to be in the regular education mainstream or have to wait for educational researchers to prove that they can profit from the mainstream while other students are allowed unrestricted access simply because they have no label. No one should have to pass any one's test, or prove anything in a research study to live and learn in the mainstream of school and community. This is a basic right, not something one has to earn. **Inclusion is not an experiment to be tested but a value to be followed.**

All children whether they are disabled or not have the right to education as they are the future citizens of the country. Inclusive education is a human right. All children have the right to learn together. Children should not be devalued or discriminated against by being excluded or sent away because of their disability. Even disabled adults describing themselves as special school survivors are demanding an end to segregation. There are no legitimate reasons to separate children for their education. Children belong together with advantages and benefits for everyone. They don't need to be protected from each other.

For a truly fair, egalitarian society in which all people are considered to have equal worth and equal rights, the school systems need to be re-evaluated. If integration and equality for all people in society is desired, then segregation in the schools cannot be justified. If we really want someone to be part of our lives we should do whatever is possible to welcome that person and accommodate his or her needs. An inclusive school welcomes everybody.

The democratic ideas of Indian society can be best served and protected when diversity is highly valued and seen as the norm in all schools, when all students are viewed as active, fully participating members of the school community. Inclusive schools value diversity and children with disability are fully participating members of such schools.

LEGAL PROVISIONS

Do the disabled have any legal rights? Do the disabled have the same legal rights as those who are not disabled? The Constitution of India applies uniformly to all citizens of India whether or not they are disabled or non-disabled.

The constitution provides the right to education to all citizens including the disabled. Article 29(2) of the Constitution provides that no citizen shall be denied admission into any educational institution maintained by the State or receiving aid out of State founds.... This also means that every child has right to receive education in an educational institution of his choice which is preferably the neighbourhood school. This also implies that every child with a disability has right to receive education in inclusive setting and the authority concerned cannot deprive the child of his right unless there are compelling reasons to do so.

Article 45 of the Constitution directs the State to provide free and compulsory education for all children (including the disabled) until they attain the age of 14 years. Recently Compulsory Primary Education Acts have been enacted by various States. This Act requires parents to send their children to school. Of course parents of disabled children may like to send their children either to special schools or to inclusive schools. Inclusive education is justified in view of financial constraints of parents to send their disabled children to special schools and/or unavailability of special schools in the neighbourhood.

Inclusion does not mean dumping disabled children into the regular classroom of the neighbourhood school. In order to serve the purpose of inclusion, disabled children must be provided with support from trained and qualified professionals. In fact, disabled children have the right to be served by trained and qualified rehabilitation professionals. Until 1992, a large number of institutions were running a variety of training programmes based on different models. There was no uniform standard. There was no control. So the Government of India decided to regulate all such training of rehabilitation professionals. For this purpose the Govt. of India enacted the Rehabilitation Council of India Act, 1992 (RCI Act, 1992).

The main objectives of the RCI Act (1992) are:

(1) To constitute the Rehabilitation Council of India as a statutory body,

(2) To regulate the training of rehabilitation professionals,

(3) To maintain a central rehabilitation register and

(4) To promote research in rehabilitation and special education.

The RCI does not function only with the objectives stated above. It looks ahead. It works for creating awareness about and promotion of inclusive education. In an interview with B.S. Padmanavan at New Delhi, Major A.P.S. Ahluwalia, Chairman of Rehabilitation Council of India stated: "The Government policy is to promote inclusive education. There are about 10 million children with disability in India and we cannot have special schools for all of them. The Government has come out with the policy of compulsory primary education for all children including those with disabilities. The Government has done its jobs but the disabled children may not go to school for two reasons":

(i) If the parents are not sensitized and are not made aware of advantages, they will not send their children to school.

(ii) If teachers are not sensitized and are not going to look at children with disabilities with understanding, what is the idea in sending these children to school.

The RCI looks at these two components. It has come to the conclusion that unless these are remedied compulsory primary education of disabled children will not come about. The RCI has developed a foundation course for elementary school teachers through distance education mode. The Indira Gandhi National Open University (IGNOU) has also launched a programme to sensitize the parents and this programme is covered under Sarva Siksha Abhiyan. Thus the RCI has taken initiative to sensitize teachers and parents so that children with disabilities can attend the inclusive school.

The Persons With Disabilities Act (1995) seeks to give effect to the proclamation on the full participation and equality of the people with disabilities in the Asian and Pacific region. The said proclamation was made at Beijing on 1st to 5th December, 1992 to launch the Asian and Pacific Decade of the Disabled Persons, 1993-2002 which was convened by Economic and Social Commission for Asian and Pacific

Region. India was a signatory to the said proclamation and therefore, it became obligatory for India to pass a suitable legislation for the benefit of the disabled. The Persons With Disabilities (Equal Opportunities, Protection of Rights and Full Participation) Act was passed in 1995 but it was made applicable to the whole of India except the State of Jammu and Kashmir with effect from July 1996.

The PWD Act (1995) spells out the responsibility of the State towards the prevention of disabilities, protection of rights, provision of medical care, education, training, employment and rehabilitation of persons with disabilities. It also provides for creating a barrier free environment for persons with disabilities, to remove any discrimination against persons with disabilities in the sharing of development benefits, to counteract any situation of the abuse and exploitation of the disabled persons, to lay down strategies for comprehensive development programmes and services, for equal opportunities for disabled persons and for their integration into the social mainstream.

So far as the education of children with disabilities is concerned the PWD Act (1995) provides:

"The appropriate Governments and local authorities shall:

(a) ensure that every child with a disability has access to free education in an appropriate environment till he attains the age of 18 years.

(b) Endeavour to promote the integration of students with disabilities in the normal schools.

(c) Promote setting up of special schools in government and private sectors for those in need of special education, in such a manner that children with disabilities living in any part of the country have access to such schools.

(d) Endeavour to equip the special schools for children with disabilities with vocational training facilities."

The PWD Act (1995) also directs the authorities to make schemes and programmes for non-formal education etc. It states:

"The appropriate Governments and local authorities shall by notification make schemes for:

(a) Conducting part-time classes in respect of children with disabilities who, having completed education up to class fifth, could not continue their studies on a whole time basis.

(b) Conducting special part-time classes for providing functional literacy for children in the age-group of sixteen and above.

(c) Imparting non-formal education by utilizing the available man-power in rural areas after giving them appropriate orientation.

(d) Imparting education through Open Schools and Open University.

(e) Conducting classes and discussions through interactive electronic or other media;

(f) Providing every child with disability, free of cost, special books and equipments needed for his education."

The PWD Act (1995) also has provision for designing and developing new assistive devices, teaching aids and special teaching materials to give disabled children equal opportunity in education. The Act has also provision to set-up teachers training institutions to prepare trained manpower for special schools and inclusive schools. Transport facilities, supply of books and uniforms, grant of scholarships, restructuring of curriculum, modifications in the examination system for benefit of disabled students and removal of architectural barriers in school, etc. are also covered under the Act.

The PWD Act (1995) provides certain right for persons with disabilities. The rights which have relevance for education in inclusive schools are as follows:

1. Right to free education in appropriate environment up to the age of 18 years.
2. Right to equal opportunity with the non-disabled.

3. Right to full participation in the activities of the school at par with those who are non-disabled.

THE BENEFITS OF INCLUSION

There are some long-held beliefs that in inclusive settings children with diverse abilities will disrupt classes and impair the learning of other children in a class, teachers will be unable to cope with the extra work expected of them, and children with diverse abilities will ultimately receive an inferior education and possibly come through the process with damaged self-esteem. But in reality, many of beliefs are founded more on preconceived notions than on any solid experience or evidence. The benefits of inclusion would seem to far outweigh any disadvantages.

Benefits of Inclusion for Children with Disabilities

McGregor and Vogelsberg (1998) list the benefits of inclusion for children with disabilities based on a comprehensive review of research literature as follows:

Children with disabilities demonstrate high levels of social interaction with non-disabled peers in inclusive settings when compared with segregated settings.

Social competence and communication skills of children with diverse abilities are improved in inclusive settings. This is believed to be closely associated with greater opportunities for social interaction with non-disabled peers.

Children with disabilities in inclusive settings often have a more rigorous educational programme, resulting in improved skill acquisition and academic gains.

Social acceptance of children with diverse abilities is enhanced by the frequent small-group work nature of their instruction in inclusive classrooms. Children get to see beyond the disability when working in small groups, and begin to realize that they have much in common with children with disabilities.

Friendships more commonly develop between children with disabilities and those without disabilities in inclusive settings. Research has found that children in inclusive settings have more durable networks of friends than children in segregated settings. This is especially true of children included in their local neighbourhood school, where they can more easily see friends outside of school hours.

Other benefits of inclusion for children with disabilities include:

Inclusion assists in the development of general knowledge for children with disabilities.

Children with disabilities who are included in regular schools tend to become adults who spend more time in leisure activities outside of the home, spend more time in leisure activities with adults without disabilities, and spend more time in community work settings than do their counterparts educated in segregated settings.

The arguments supporting inclusion are compelling. The opposing argument that children with diverse abilities receive an inferior standard of education in an inclusive setting, or are somehow socially disadvantaged, is difficult to sustain.

Benefits of Inclusion for Children without Disabilities

In many ways children without disabilities benefit from inclusion just as much as children with diverse abilities. The following benefits of inclusion for children without disabilities have been substantiated in the literature:

The performance of children without disabilities or giftedness is not compromised by the presence of children with diverse abilities in their classes.

The perception that children with diverse abilities can disrupt a class is largely unsubstantiated in the research literature.

Children without disabilities or giftedness can benefit from improved instructional technologies in the classroom. Other children can benefit from the presence of these technologies, and can use them when they are not required by the child with diverse abilities.

Children without disabilities or giftedness can benefit from increased funds in the classroom. Extra funds and resources removed from 'special programmes' can be used in the regular classroom to enhance the learning of both children with diverse abilities and their peers.

Children without disabilities or giftedness benefit from higher classroom staff ratios. Frequently, extra funding for children with diverse abilities is directed towards the provision of additional staff, either specialist teachers or para-professionals. In either case, the presence of an extra adult in the classroom opens up a wide range of possibilities for all children.

Children without disabilities or giftedness involved in peer-tutoring situations can benefit from improved self-esteem and mastery of academic content. Furthermore, it has been found that peer tutors demonstrate a higher mastery of academic content in a given area than do their peers who are not involved as tutors.

Children without disabilities or giftedness have the opportunity to learn additional skills such as Braille or sign language. These skills can be taught in a meaningful context and represent an opportunity for growth not often available to children who are not educated with others with diverse abilities (McGregor and Vogelsberg, 1998).

Children without disabilities or giftedness can learn to value and respect children with diverse abilities in inclusive classrooms. They learn to see past the disability or giftedness and the associated social stigmas when placed in inclusive classes.

5

Innovative Practices in Inclusive Settings

The World Declaration on Education for All, Jomtien, Thailand, which was reaffirmed in the Dakar Frame Work for Action (2000), gives the message:

"In order to attract and retain children from marginalized and excluded groups, education systems should respond flexibly. Education systems must be inclusive, actively seeking out children who are not enrolled, and responding flexibly to the circumstances and needs of all learners...."

The World Conferences on Special Needs Education, Salamanca calls on the international communities to endorse inclusive education (to achieve the goal of Education for All) and to support the development of special needs education as an integral part of all education programmes.

Inclusive education does not mean dumping children with special needs into the regular classroom. We have to accept their diversity, respect their individuality, create opportunity for their participation in all activities of the school and provide support to both children and teachers so that children can realize their full potential and teachers will be able to improve their performance. This calls for, among other things, a change in teaching practices, a shift from traditional teaching styles to innovative practices in inclusive settings. Five innovative practices are presented here. These are:

- Peer Tutoring
- Cooperative Learning
- Collaboration, Consultation and Team Teaching

- Curriculum Adaptation
- Individualized Education Programme

PEER TUTORING

What is Peer Tutoring?

Tutoring is a process that involves one-to-one instruction. It can involve a peer, an older student or an expert teacher in the tutoring role. The tutor is the individual who provides instruction, and the tutee is the one who receives instruction. Tutoring can be used to meet the special education needs of children by providing remedial or supportive instruction. Of all types of tutoring peer tutoring is the most effective in inclusive settings.

Peer tutoring is instruction provided by the peers of students. It means children teaching other children usually on a one-to-one basis. It may be *cross-age tutoring* or *same-age tutoring*. Cross-age tutoring refers to instructional situation in which the peer-tutor provides instruction to younger children of a lower grade. Same-age tutoring refers to instruction that involves children of the same age or grade in the tutoring process. Whatever type of peer tutoring is adopted, it can be used for teaching spelling, hand-writing, arithmetic and social behaviour in the last period and twice a week.

Goals for Peer Tutoring

The goals of peer tutoring may be in the academic (cognitive), social or psycho-motor domains.

Cognitive domain—To teach a set of cognitive skills (e.g., spelling, arithmetic, etc.) to the child with SEN.

Social domain—To improve the tutee's social behaviour (e.g., cooperation, friendship, mutual respect and acceptance).

Psycho-motor domain—To teach improved handwriting skills.

Whatever may be the goals, peer tutoring should not be viewed as a substitute for classroom instruction. The peer tutor should not be also considered as a substitute for regular teachers. The peer tutor has to play a supportive role by providing remedial instruction, additional practice, modeling, etc.

Tutoring Procedures

Peer tutors should be oriented about the tutoring procedures before they are actually engaged in tutorial activities. There are basically three tutoring procedures:

- The show-do procedure,
- Test-teach-test procedure, and
- Paired teaching procedure.

The show-do activity is a routine procedure that entails demonstrating the task, then asking the tutee to complete the same task. It is a very strait forward modeling procedure that nearly all tutors have little difficulty in learning. The first principle that tutors should apply is that they should teach in small steps, one at a time and also provide clear demonstrations of the way that students can link the steps together. The second principle is for tutors to ensure that students practise immediately after each task or step has been demonstrated. Students must show the tutor that they can complete each step of the required task in the required sequence.

The test-teach-test procedure involves a three-step process. First the tutor tests to see if the tutee can do the required task. If the tutee fails, then the task is analyzed to see what particular aspects of the task are causing difficulty. The second step is the instructional phase. This is the same as the show-do procedure. During the third step, the tutee is tested to see if the task has been mastered. If not, the student's response is again analyzed for errors and the instructional procedure is repeated. Sometimes, the tutee partially completes the task, but is unable to satisfy the prescribed mastery criteria.

The paired teaching procedure involves the tutor and tutee taking turns to complete activities. The tutor does the first of the assignment tasks, and the tutee does the second, then the tutor does the third and so on until the assignment has been completed. For example, in an oral reading exercise the tutor might read the first passage, the tutee the second and so on until the task is completed. The tutee usually models aspects of the behaviour of the tutor (e.g., elements of phrasing in reading). This routine works successfully if the curriculum material is well-graded and matches the tutee's abilities.

Peer Tutoring

In peer tutoring the tutor should perform four acts, such as:

- **Monitoring** (Supervision and regulation of the performance of a tutee).
- **Reinforcing** (Providing appropriate contingencies for approved behaviour).
- **Modeling** (demonstration of a particular activity or behaviour).
- **Explaining** (exposing the relationships, providing appropriate examples, clarifying doubts on a topic).

The success of peer tutoring depends upon the interpersonal and communicative relationships between peers. In peer tutoring, although the tutor plays an important role in the instructional process, it is the teacher who virtually retains overall responsibility for selecting the tutors, orienting them about their crucial role, matching the tutor with the tutee, directing, organizing, coordinating and evaluating the performance of the tutorial project. The teacher should follow the guidelines given in Box 5.1 for establishing a peer tutoring programme.

Box 5.1: Guidelines for Peer Tutoring Programme

(i) Make a careful diagnosis of the tutee's weakness in the subject area.

(ii) Inform the tutor about the levels of mastery expected for the tutee and the timeframe (Tutoring should not be viewed as a time-filling exercise).

(iii) Match the tutor and the tutee. (The tutor must have mastery over the subject and skills to be learned by the tutee. Pairing of tutor and the tutee should be based on similar interests and background and sometimes on sex. It may be a good practice to give both the tutor and the tutee some choice in the selection of partners).

(iv) Develop appropriate instructional packages, worksheets, games and learning activities, charts, record sheets and other practice materials in advance that can be used by the tutor.

(v) Arrange a short training programme for tutors which should include tutoring skills, giving feedback, questioning, student management etc. This can be done through explicit instruction, guidance, modeling or watching experts.

(vi) Establish a practical work routine and suitable work environment for tutoring.

(vii) Reinforce both the tutor and the tutee and encourage them to persist at the prescribed task.

(viii) Monitor the progress of tutoring in terms of concepts and skills to be learned, quality of relationship and communication between the tutor and the tutee, attendance and completion of tasks.

(ix) Change the tutor, if there is conflict between the tutor and the tutee or if there is personal animosity or dissatisfaction in the tutoring situations.

(x) Give certificate of merit to the tutor and some incentives to the tutee if the tutoring programme has been completed successfully.

Source: Dash, M. (2002): "Classroom for All" in *Orientation Package for Teacher Educators*, New Delhi, NCERT, p. 40.

Advantages and Limitations

Peer tutoring has been a favoured practice in inclusive settings due to its potential advantages.

Peer tutoring benefits children with special needs and all other children. It has the potential to deliver many of the benefits normally associated with expert tutoring by teachers. If teachers organize the contents of the programme peer tutors can provide appropriate activities tailored to meet the individual needs of children with special needs. They can ensure a high level of tutee participation in the learning process, and individual guidance and personal care can be provided. Coverage of subject content is normally guaranteed. Tutors can devote full attention to the tutees and classroom teachers can concentrate the major part of their time to the other students in their classes. Other advantages are as follows:

Tutors can effectively monitor learning and routine assignments. Each step in the learning process can be supervised and mistakes identified and corrected. In one-to-one tutoring situation it is relatively easy to identify incorrect responses as soon as they are made and to supply the necessary correctives if needed. Individual feedback can be provided at the time it is most needed. Additional demonstrations or explanations can also be provided by the tutor or supervising teacher if extensive reteaching is required. The peer tutor is also able to employ the most effective reinforcers and use those at the most appropriate times.

Tutoring normally promotes healthy social relationships between students with special needs and their peer tutors. It also encourages positive interaction between regular class students and those with special needs, and allows individuals to work together in cooperative work environments. Peer tutoring encourages close personal relationships, personal interdependence and shared responsibility for learning outcomes. Since peer tutoring removes or reduces deficiencies in children with special needs, such children become active and participate in many regular class activities. This makes the learning environment competitive and thus stimulates higher levels of attainment.

Although there are many advantages of peer tutoring programme, few limitations of peer tutoring may make it a failure. The quality of interpersonal relationships and the degree of communication between the tutor and the tutee are affected when tutors are asked to instruct too many tutees. Management problems can also cause difficulties for the tutor in those situations. If the relationships between the tutor and the tutee lead to conflict situations the tutoring situation has little chance of success. Peer tutoring requires the tutor to be adequately trained in the art of tutoring. If the tutor is not properly trained then it is difficult to achieve the goal and it becomes simply a waste of time and energy. Few critics also question the advantages of peer tutoring over expert tutoring by experienced and competent teachers. But as long as expert tutoring is not feasible in our schools, peer tutoring can be accepted as a supportive technique in inclusive settings.

COOPERATIVE LEARNING

What is Cooperative Learning?

In an inclusive classroom where a large number of children with and without SEN have been enrolled, children can be taught with the help of cooperative learning techniques. In this way, the children help each other learn, they work together to seek solutions to problems and to complete the assignment.

Cooperative learning is a procedure used by a mixed ability group to achieve a common goal with mutual collaboration and support. Cooperative learning provides opportunities to children to learn academic skills and pro-social skills of listening, taking turns, asking questions, seeking assistance, answering questions, offering suggestions, good manners, speaking positively about others and correcting others. The teacher operates as a planner, facilitator and evaluator. He has to ensure that:

- the child takes responsibility for his or her own learning;
- there is focused interaction between each of the members of the group;

- each member of the group helps other members to learn and
- each member uses sound social skills and group processes to solve problems.

Cooperative Learning

Goals of Cooperative Learning

Cooperative learning in inclusive settings has the following goals:

- To give opportunity to the child with special needs to learn academic skills in a cooperative learning situation;
- To create situation where the child with special needs learns pro-social skills;
- To encourage the child to take responsibility for his or her own learning;
- To facilitate social interaction between each of the members of the cooperative group;
- To ensure that children with and without disability develop friendship and
- To develop their problem solving skills through mutual collaboration and support.

Guidelines for Cooperative Learning

The teacher should follow the guidelines given in Box 5.2 to organize the programme.

Box 5.2: Guidelines for Cooperative Learning

(i) The teacher should specify the instructional objectives of the lesson.
(ii) He should place children in groups.
(iii) Each group should be small in size and heterogeneous.
(iv) He should arrange the room or the learning environment in such a way that groups are not too close or too far. The members of the group should sit together facing each other to facilitate interaction.
(v) He should assign roles to each member of the group- leader, recorder, performer and evaluator.
(vi) He should rotate roles by lessons so that each member of the group has the opportunity to lead, record, perform and evaluate.
(vii) He should explain the task to the group and distribute materials.
(viii) He should ensure individual accountability. That is, even if children work cooperatively, each child has to take responsibility for his/her own learning.
(ix) He should ensure interaction among group members without which cooperative learning is meaningless.
(x) He should monitor the progress of individual children and the group and provide assistance to the group whenever it is needed.
(xi) He should evaluate the performance of individual children and the group as a whole in terms of :
    Level of mastery,
    Completion of task,
    Quality and quantity of work done,
    Peer interaction and collaboration,
    Satisfaction of the group as a whole.
(xii) Cooperative learning should begin with younger children so that they learn collaborative skills early and progress effectively in later grades.

Source: Dash, M. (2002): *Classroom for All In Orientation Package on Inclusive Education for Teacher Educators*, New Delhi, NCERT – pp. 40-41.

Advantages and Limitations

Cooperative learning has certain advantages. It benefits not only the special needs children but also other children. It promotes individual accountability for learning. It is a convenient way for helping the special needs child to learn academic and social skills. When children with and without disability learn together they also learn to live together in the community. In a cooperative learning situation children learn to accept and respect diversity and develop friendship. The child with special needs learns that he has much in common with other children in the group.

Cooperative learning ensures interaction among members of the group. "Such interactions generate new concepts. The special needs child learns to assimilate the concepts into his existing cognitive structure. If required, he also reconstructs his cognitive structure to accommodate the new concepts. All this helps to expand his cognitive structures. The child is now able to act upon the world in more flexible and complex ways" (Piaget, 1999).

Cooperative learning takes a lot of time of the teacher for planning and organizing the group for which teachers are not interested to adopt this strategy. If the teacher fails to guide the group members properly, the purpose will be lost and the entire process will be a mess.

COLLABORATION AND CONSULTATION

Collaboration is essential for meaningful inclusion to occur. Collaboration is essentially a process whereby participating teachers develop shared meanings and/or a shared agenda, and then, in a cooperative way set out to implement that agenda. This can be achieved through positive interactions, consultation and communication. In fact the success of any collaboration depends on high quality consultation and communication.

Collaboration can be *indirect collaboration* or *direct collaboration*. Indirect collaboration refers to working with the teacher outside of the classroom to plan for student needs. Collaborative consultation, peer collaboration and teacher assistance teams are forms of indirect collaboration. Co-operative teaching or co-teaching or team teaching refers to direct collaboration. A description of various types of collaborative efforts is given in Box 5.3.

Box 5.3: Types of Collaborative Efforts

Approach	*Nature of Contact with Student*	*Description*
Collaborative Consultation	Indirect	General education teacher requests the services of the special education teacher to help generate ideas for addressing an on-going situation.
Peer Collaboration	Indirect	The regular education teachers work together to identify effective solutions to classroom situations.
Teacher Assistance Team	Indirect	A team of teachers provide support to general education teachers in analyzing the problem and developing potential solutions.
Co-operative Teaching	Direct	General and special education teachers work together in providing direct service to students.

Prerequisites for Collaboration

Collaboration with colleagues can occur at any stage or for any purpose—planning, problem-solving, teaching, evaluation or even assessment. But collaboration does not occur automatically. Friend and Cook (1996) identified a number of prerequisites for collaboration to occur. These include:

(i) Collaboration should be voluntary. People can be forced to meet but they can not be forced to truly collaborate. Collaboration involves willing parties coming together to achieve a common goal.

(ii) Collaboration requires parity between participants. All members of a collaboration team must be seen as equal. This promotes a freedom for all members of the team to provide, process and evaluate ideas and information. This does not preclude members of a team taking leadership roles in different areas. Rather it means that all contributions are considered equal regardless of whom they come from.

(iii) Collaboration presumes mutually agreed-on goals. Members of a collaborative team must work towards a clearly articulated common goal or goals.

(iv) Collaboration requires shared responsibility and shared resources. All members of the group must be a part of the process of arriving at and agreeing on decisions. In this way the decision will be supported. Resources to achieve team goals should be available to all members of a collaborative team as required.

(v) Team members must be collectively responsible for the outcomes of their decisions. This means that all team members share the success or failure of any collaborative effort. No single individual should be singled out for credit or blame. This helps collaborative teams to work together.

In addition to the above prerequisites is the condition that collaboration should not lead to finding fault with any teacher. It should not lead to evaluating or judging ideas or suggestions in a negative way. Comments, if any, should be positively oriented at helping the team to arrive at a solution.

Benefits of Collaboration

The benefits of collaboration with other teachers are many and may include:

- the development of ideas a teacher might not have thought of;
- using limited resources so that demand is not placed on them at the same time;
- a critique of his teaching plans resulting in a more 'robust' programme;
- reduced work—the teacher can use ideas from the lesson plan of others and they can use his ideas;
- a more enjoyable, social planning experience;
- development of a support network;
- a greater awareness of what is occurring in other classes and
- assistance with context—dependent problem-solving.

TEAM TEACHING

What is Team Teaching?

In inclusive settings where children with and without disabilities are educated regular education teachers feel defeated to teach. They lack confidence. This is perhaps one reason why regular education teachers are hesitant to include special needs children in their classrooms. Team teaching is a positive step towards helping teachers to face the challenge.

Team teaching refers to an instructional situation in which two or more teachers join together, plan together, teach together and evaluate together. It can be done in a variety of ways, but involves both general and special education teachers working together in the classroom and instructing the entire class. The least restrictive approach is co-teaching, where both teachers teach together at the same time or switch subjects or topics. Other team teaching approaches involve small group work as well as individual tutorial or assistance to make classroom experiences successful.

Goals of Team Teaching

- To make best use of attractive abilities, expertise and interests of teachers;
- To make classroom instruction more effective to meet the needs of children;
- To enhance the quality of instruction;
- To increase/develop teachers' confidence while teaching children with special needs;
- To remove the feeling of isolation of regular education teachers in inclusive settings and
- To ensure cooperation and collaboration between regular education teachers and special education teacher.

Procedure of Team Teaching

Team teaching relieves teachers from the tension arising in inclusive settings provided it is planned carefully, implemented systematically and evaluated objectively. The guidelines given in Box 5.4 are important.

Box 5.4: Guidelines for Team Teaching

(i) Assess the present knowledge of the child with special needs and other children;
(ii) Decide the topic for teaching and prepare an outline;
(iii) Determine the objectives of team teaching;
(iv) Assign duties and responsibilities among special education teacher and regular education teacher or among the team members;
(v) Determine the level of instruction;
(vi) Decide the evaluation techniques;
(vii) Start team teaching as per planning. The regular teacher or one teacher delivers the lead lecture and the other teacher or the special education teacher listens to it;
(viii) The other member of the team or the special education teacher notes down important points which need further explanation and clarifies doubts;
(ix) Now ask children including those with special needs to perform certain tasks and reinforce their performance;
(x) Evaluate their achievements in terms of objectives framed earlier through oral and written questions and practical assignments;
(xi) Provide remedial instruction, if required; and
(xii) Bring modifications and improvements in the planning and implementation, if needed.

Advantages and Limitations

Team teaching approach lends itself to flexibility in delivery of instruction depending on the lesson and children's needs. The advantage of team teaching over consultation is the ability to modify and adapt, as needed, on the spot.

Team teaching creates confidence and contributes to quality instruction. If a special education teacher or any member of the team possesses strength or interest in a particular area he will typically be more comfortable teaching this subject.

While team teaching is successful and positive some teachers may not be comfortable with it. The co-teachers may not hold the same belief systems. In this case, it is not a comfortable work environment for teachers or students.

CURRICULUM ADAPTATION

Curriculum is central to the teaching and learning that occurs in inclusive schools. In broad terms it has to do with the teaching and learning of knowledge, skills and attitudes. It refers to the totality of learning experiences in and outside the classrooms.

When teaching learners with diverse abilities, curriculum can be divided into two broad areas. These are 'core curriculum' and 'elaborative curriculum'. Core curriculum consists of areas judged to be basic and essential for all learners. The term 'elaborative curriculum' relates to all other aspects of curriculum that could be considered 'non-core'. The elaborative curriculum is important as it adds richness, depth, scope and variety to the core curriculum. What constitutes core curriculum and what constitutes elaborative curriculum is context dependent and depends on the views, attitudes and values of everyone involved in the educational process. For some, learning of fine art or music would be seen as non-essential and, therefore, could be classified as elaborative curriculum. For others, they are classified as core curriculum. In inclusive settings, the learning of children with diverse abilities should be based on a mixture of both the core curriculum and elaborative curriculum.

We know of no country in the world in which the regular curriculum is appropriate for all students. While most education systems claim that their curriculum is appropriate for all, this is never the case unless some form of curriculum adaptation takes place. While good instructional design for the entire class can minimize the need for adaptations, sometimes the only way to cater for children with special needs is to adapt the curriculum in order to accommodate their learning goals.

In inclusive schools the focus is not on how to help all children to gain access to the existing curriculum of the school. Rather the focus is on adapting the curriculum to fit to the needs of any student. In other words, the instructional objectives may be same for all students, but the learning experiences may be different for different children when needed. For example, while most students in a science unit on temperature may focus on learning to understand Fahrenheit and Celsius temperature scales, one student with visual impairment may learn to recognize and point to items that are hot and cold. That is, while all students can pursue the same basic educational goals (what is temperature) and learn together in the same regular education class, it may be necessary for some students to pursue the same goal by a different approach and be evaluated differently.

Curriculum can be adapted in various ways such as:

- Adapting the materials/contents
- Adapting teaching strategies
- Adapting the level of support
- Adapting the rules
- Substituting the curriculum

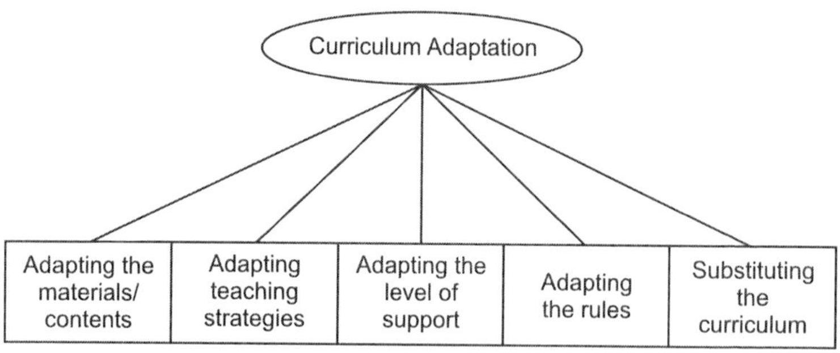

Adapting the Materials/Contents

In modern classrooms learning materials are predominantly language-oriented. Some children with disabilities have difficulty in reading, and writing. Thus the first suggestion is to increase the readability of written passages. For some children adaption will be in the form of enlarging the print, for others it will be double spacing. Measures such as these will make the materials 'user friendly' and the comprehension process easier. Deepeler (1998) outlines the ways to adapt the materials which are given in Box 5.5.

Box 5.5: Ways to Adapt the Material

(i) Increase the readability.
(ii) Highlight critical features.
(iii) Reduce extraneous details and simplify the layout.
(iv) Supplement with visual cues (pictures, diagrams, maps, illustrations).
(v) Supplement with written cues and prompts.
(vi) Reduce the contents (amount of materials).
(vii) Simplify the language (use shorter sentences and simpler vocabulary).
(viii) Include selected content (essential content, experience based or interest based).
(ix) Use alternative materials (models, videos, etc.).
(x) Create new materials.
(xi) Use student work folder for daily assignments.

Adapting Teaching Strategies

An important aspect of curriculum adaptation is adapting teaching strategies to fit to the needs of children with diverse abilities. Instruction can be adapted in various ways which are given in Box 5.6.

Box 5.6: Ways to Adapt Teaching Strategies

(i) Use modeling and direct instruction.
(ii) Provide additional demonstrations using step by step approach.
(iii) Provide concrete experiences as far as possible.
(iv) Set more practice items and provide guided practice with frequent feedback.
(v) Give positive feedback such as praise.
(vi) Use co-operative learning, peer tutoring, co-teaching and individualized education programmes.
(vii) Use a variety of modes for learning activities. Do not rely on passive listening. Encourage active learning.
(viii) Change the pace of instruction. Increase wait time for oral responses, shorten instruction, and repeat key elements.
(ix) Ask more questions and use different levels of complexity.
(x) Provide hints or clues to facilitate students' responses.
(xi) Use audio-visual aids.

Adapting the Level of Support

Some children with special needs require more support from the teacher or peers. Thus the teacher may adapt the level of support by increasing the amount of personal assistance.

Peers may also be involved to provide academic support to a child.

Adapting the Rules

The teacher may adapt the rules relating to how a learner should approach the work by allowing the use of a calculator to solve problems in arithmetic, changing or simplifying directions or allowing the child to respond to questions orally instead of answering the questions in writing. He may also allow extra time to complete the task or answer the questions during examinations. (See Box 5.7)

Box 5.7: Adapting the Rules

(i) Allow the use of calculator to solve problems in arithmetic;
(ii) Change directions/instruction;
(iii) Simplify directions/ instruction;
(iv) Allow the child to respond to questions orally instead of giving the answers in writing or the vice versa and
(v) Allow extra time to complete the assignment or answer questions during examinations.

Substituting the Curriculum

Sometimes, a child with special needs may require the curriculum substituted for him. For example, a child with hearing loss has difficulty with language test. The teacher may substitute the curriculum for him by asking him to learn computer skills during the language test.

INDIVIDUALIZED EDUCATION PROGRAMME (IEP)

What is IEP?

Individualized education programme (IEP) refers to a carefully designed, systematically implemented and objectively evaluated programme to meet the special education needs of an individual child. Individual programmes for special needs children help educators to ensure that these children are making progress in schools. Well written individual programmes also help a teacher to systematically structure and sequence learning in specifically targeted areas. This is not to say that everything a child learns at school will or should be included in an individual plan. Rather individual programmes provide a focus point for the main emphasis of a child's learning over a specified period of time. Used properly they can be an excellent aid to teaching on a daily basis.

Purposes of IEP

The purposes of IEP are to ensure:

- some degree of accountability for teachers to meet the needs of the individual child,
- adequate communication among all persons within the school and between school and home concerning the child,
- reducing the deficiencies in the child,
- developing competency of the child in the focused area,
- behaviour modification and
- developing/improving the adaptive behaviour of the child.

Whose Responsibility?

IEP is a complex process. It is not the responsibility of any single person. Just as successful inclusion depends upon a number of persons who are concerned with the welfare of the child with special needs, so also IEP involves a group of persons. It is the joint responsibility of this group of professionals who constitute the IEP team. In most westernized countries the headmaster, the regular education teacher or the class teacher, the special educator or the resource teacher, the parent(s) of the child and specialist doctor/the psychologist constitute the IEP team. In our country specialist doctors or the psychologists are not always available in schools for conducting assessment of the child. In such circumstances should we not go for individual programme for the child with special needs? To begin with, the IEP team in Indian schools may constitute the following members and whenever and wherever specialist doctors and psychologists are available we can utilize their services.

The IEP Team

Components of IEP

The IEP should contain the following components:

(i) A statement of the present level of performance of the child,

(ii) A statement of annual goals including short-term objectives for the child,

(iii) A statement of the specific educational services to be provided to each child and the extent to which each child will be able to participate in regular education programme,

(iv) The projected date for initiation and anticipated duration of such services and

(v) Appropriate evaluation procedures and schedules for determining whether instructional objectives are being achieved.

Steps of IEP

Generally speaking IEP proceeds through the following steps:

Step 1: Referral

The child is referred as may be needing special services. The referral must be in written form and may be made by anyone involved with the child (parents, teachers, etc.). If the referral is made by the teacher, then the parents should be informed in writing about the referral.

Step 2: Assessment

Assessment is the systematic process of gathering educationally relevant information about the child. The purpose is to know what the child can do and what he cannot do, his strengths, limitations and the problems. Assessment may be any one of the following three or even all the three types:

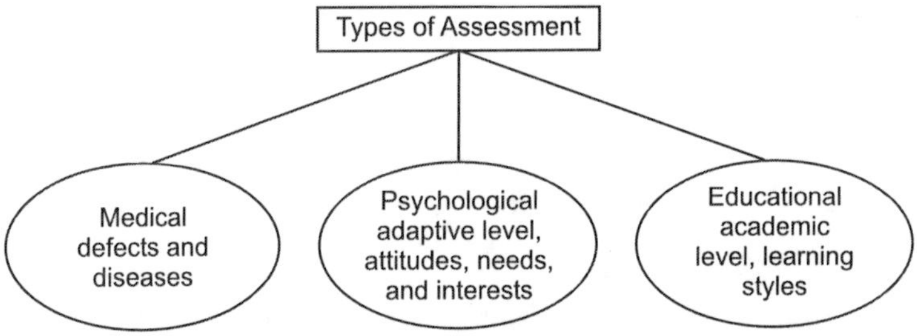

Medical assessment can indicate the child's defects and diseases, if any, which may adversely affect his functioning level. Psychological assessment will reveal the adaptive level, attitudes and interests, etc. of the child. Educational assessment will present a clear picture about the present level of academic assessment and learning styles of the child.

For conducting assessment the child's records are reviewed for any information already available. The committee chairperson decides if more information is needed so that possible services can be discussed and, if so, what information is needed. If enough information is already available a committee meeting will be held to discuss the assessment report. If no information is available or if the information already available is not adequate then fresh assessment will be made.

The assessment team should be multi-disciplinary. It should be non-discriminatory, i.e., not biased by race, culture, socio-economic status or any impairment. After the assessment is made a committee meeting should be held to discuss the assessment report. The parents should decide whether they believe the assessment reports are appropriate, right, good or correct. If the parents do not accept the report they may go for independent assessment conducted by someone other than the school.

Step 3: Programme Planning

After the assessment is over, the committee should now plan individual programme for the child. It should state annual goals and short-term objectives on monthly or quarterly basis. The committee should decide the specific educational services to be provided (such as, speech training, remedial instruction etc.). The committee should also decide who will be responsible for providing services, what services are required, where the services will be provided, when the services should start, how and why it will be provided, the materials required for the purpose, the time frame, etc.

Step 4: Implementation

After the programme is planned systematically, the services should now begin as per planning.

Step 5: Evaluation

Evaluation of the services should be an integral part of the implementation process. It should be objective-based. Evaluation can be conducted monthly or quarterly or annually. It should indicate whether the child is making satisfactory progress and, if not, what changes are required in the service delivery.

Step 6: Completion

The services should continue until the committee decides that they are no longer required. The IEP comes to an end if the goals are achieved in terms of behaviour modification or improvement of academic standard or development of adaptive behaviour, etc.

Values of IEP

The individualized education programme has values not only for the child with special needs but also for teachers and parents.

In the traditional approach to teaching, teachers are not accountable for the failure of the child. But IEP ensures some degree of accountability for teachers.

In the traditional system there is no linkage between the home and the school, parents and teachers. Usually teachers work in isolation of others. The IEP promotes communication and collaboration among the regular education teacher and the special education teacher. Inclusive education requires partnership between teachers and parents. The IEP ensures involvement of parents in the education and welfare of their children.

In traditionally oriented programme there is no scope to remove or reduce the deficiencies in the child. The IEP reduces the deficiencies in the child and develops his competency in the focused area.

The IEP ensures modification of undesirable behaviour of the child and helps him to learn desirable behaviour and improve his adaptive behaviour.

Some Difficulties

IEP is a very rare feature in Indian schools. Even special schools providing education to children with disabilities are not able to implement IEP. The following are some of the difficulties for which our schools are not in a position to adopt IEP.

Teachers are not trained in the theory and practice of IEP. IEP does not find place in pre-service and in-service teacher education programmes in our country. Even if it is there, it is not given due emphasis.

Most of the teacher educators do not possess command over the programme.

Professionals such as specialist doctors, psychologists, rehabilitation personnel, etc. are not readily available to form IEP team.

Head masters lack leadership.

Parents, in most cases, are not involved in any decision-making relating to assessment and education of their child.

IEP is a time consuming process. It requires enough patience. But our parents are too ambitious. They expect too much too soon.

There is no clear direction from the Government to schools for implementing IEP.

Barriers, Failures and Interventions

6

BARRIERS TO INCLUSION

Attitudes

Attitudes are basic and pervasive aspects of human life. Our attitudes clearly affect our thoughts, our feelings, and what we do. They actually determine what we think, feel and do. Allport (1954) suggested that an attitude is basically a readiness to respond in a particular kind of way, but attitudes also are very emotional, because they reflect the ways we evaluate people and things. They guide us in deciding whether we like or dislike someone or something and whether we are going to approach or avoid that person or thing.

The greatest barrier to inclusion is the attitude of teachers. If teachers hold unfavourable or negative attitude towards inclusion of children with special needs in the regular classroom, if they possess negative beliefs about the educability of such children in the regular schools then inclusion will not be successful.

In certain cases attitude of parents of non-disabled children also creates bottlenecks. Some parents are not in favour of sending their children to schools where both disabled and non-disabled children learn together, on the grounds that the education of their children will be affected by including disabled children in the regular class and that their children will imitate the undesirable behaviours and manners of disabled children.

Attitude of teachers can be changed by exposing them to inclusion practices, in service education programmes, workshops and seminars, literature in the field and by learning from others' experiences. Similarly, attitude of parents can also be changed through awareness programmes.

Labeling

In most cases regular teachers tend to categorize and address such children by a label. Inclusion does not accept labels of any kind. Labeling is not a healthy practice in inclusive settings for a number of reasons. Some of these negative effects of labeling are:

- Labels usually focus on a child's negative aspects. Once a child is labeled, teachers tend to think about the child only in terms of his/her inadequacies or defects. Labels such as *langra, andha, behra*, etc. are barriers to inclusion.
- Teachers and parents tend to have low expectations about what a child can do. Expectations of teachers and parents are usually reflected in children's performances.
- Teachers tend to explain a child's poor performance only in terms of his defects, and not in terms of instructional failure.
- A labeled child develops a poor self-concept.
- Labels lead to rejection by the peers.
- Labels create a sense of helplessness, inferiority and stigmatization.

Peer Rejection

Children with special needs may be enrolled in the regular class, but they may not be accepted and respected by their age-peers. Under this circumstance, the child with a disability may be teased and bullied by his peers. This acts as a major barrier to inclusion. Peer rejection can be avoided by encouraging children to develop friendships.

Teachers' Respect for Diversity

Inclusion values diversity-not-assimilation. Teachers should, therefore, respect the diversity among children and provide programmes keeping in view their individuality. Lack of teachers' respect for diversity is a barrier to inclusion.

Partnership

We must realize that the whole foundation of inclusion of children having SEN in the community and community institutions like the schools rests on building partnership. No one person can achieve as much as can be achieved through the team efforts. Partnerships between teachers and parents, regular education teachers and special education teacher, school and the community is an essential condition for the success of inclusion. If this partnership is missing, inclusion will not be successful.

Accountability

When a special needs child is placed in the regular school he/she is considered to be the sole responsibility of the special education teacher. If the school does not have a special education teacher then he is no body's responsibility. No one is accountable for his education. Lack of accountability of teachers is a barrier to successful inclusion. In fact, education of special needs children in inclusive settings should be the responsibility of each and every teacher. Every teacher related to the education of such children should be accountable to the community.

Traditionally Oriented Teaching

Children with diverse abilities have unique needs. They need an instruction which will meet their special needs. But in most cases teachers follow traditional approach to teaching such children. There are teachers in schools who follow the whole class lecture method with a fixed time table, a single text book and rigid age grouping. Curriculum is not adapted to meet their needs. Their instruction is focused on the whole class and individual attention is not paid to children. True inclusion will not be successful unless teachers modify their approach to teaching. Traditional teaching is a barrier to providing quality education to children with special needs in inclusive settings. In-service education programmes can help teachers to adopt innovative practices to meet the unique needs of children with diverse abilities and contribute to their efficiency in inclusive settings.

Integration of Personnel and Resources

Effective inclusion requires that the school personnel and resources should be integrated. All teachers and resources of the school should be available for providing services to children with diverse abilities. An unhealthy division between special education personnel and resources and the regular education personnel and resources is a barrier to effective inclusion. In order to overcome this barrier all teachers should be considered as teachers of the school and all children with and without disabilities should be viewed as learners waiting to be taught.

Collaboration/Consultation

Teaching special needs children in inclusive setting is not as simple as it may appear. Teachers may not be able to deal with the situation individually. There is, thus, a necessity of collaboration and consultation among teachers. Lack of collaboration and consultation is a barrier to provide quality education to children with special needs.

Lack of Support

Special needs children who are included in the regular classrooms require support from teachers and peers to make satisfactory progress in learning. If they don't get the support they may experience failure and later drop-out from school. This defeats the very purpose of inclusion and consequently the inclusion process will also fail.

Involvement of Parents and Community

A crucial barrier to effective inclusion is non-involvement of parents and community in the process of inclusion. In most cases parents send their children to school but they are not involved in any aspect of inclusion such as assessment, decision-making and education of their children. They are alienated from the school. Moreover, a lot depends on community participation. Non-involvement of parents and community may act as a barrier to successful inclusion. Community awareness programmes and parent-contact programmes will motivate parents and community for their involvement in the process of inclusion.

Linkage with Special Schools

Inclusion of children with special needs in the regular schools does not mean closing down an unacceptable system of special schools. Rather special schools with their expert teachers and special aids and equipments should function as resource centres for inclusive schools. Children enrolled in inclusive schools who need specialized help may be referred to special schools or that specialist teachers working in special school may be requested to provide special assistance and services to such children. For this purpose, there should be linkage between special schools and the inclusive schools. When this linkage is not established, the child with special needs loses the game. Lack of linkage between special schools and inclusive schools is a barrier to inclusion.

Leadership of the Headmaster

Lack of leadership of the headmaster acts as a barrier to effective inclusion. Headmasters are expected to possess the knowledge, attitude, leadership qualities, initiatives and resourcefulness to guide his colleagues in the art and science of inclusive education. They need to develop conceptual clarity about inclusion, the objectives to be achieved and the activities to be organized in the school. When teachers face difficulties they naturally look to the headmaster for help. If headmasters lack leadership qualities they will not be in a position to guide their colleagues; they will not be able to command respect from the colleagues and the community. Every aspect of inclusion—enrolment, retention, identification, assessment, curricular and co-curricular activities, learner friendly evaluation, in fact, everything depends on the expertise and initiative of the headmaster. If inclusion fails or becomes ineffective it is the headmaster who is to be blamed first.

EDUCATIONAL FAILURE OF SPECIAL NEEDS CHILDREN

Some teachers may have the belief that children with special needs are not capable of learning the school related subjects. A study conducted by Dash (2005) has revealed that special needs children experience severe difficulties in basic academic skills such as reading, writing and arithmetic as reported by the regular education teachers. Such children experience generalized failure and show below average performance in content areas as reported by regular education teachers. Why do special needs children experience educational failure? How can their educational failure be reduced?

Causes of Educational Failure of Special Needs Children

In the study conducted by Dash (2005) regular teachers and resource teachers were asked to indicate the causes of failure of children with special needs. This study has revealed that regular teachers have identified the deficits within the child such as:

- Lack of motivation,
- Deficit work habits,
- Poor interpersonal relationships and communication skills and
- Passive academic involvement.

The factors responsible for failure of such children as reported by resource teachers are:

- Teachers' failure to recognize student's needs and difficulties,
- Teaching methods not responsive to student's characteristics,
- Instruction not individualized,
- Personal help not given by teachers,
- Extra time needed by the student not allowed,
- Remedial instruction not given by the teachers,
- Student's progress not monitored by the teachers,

- Supportive learning environment not created in the class and
- Lack of parental care, encouragement and help.

If you ask regular class teachers why students fail to learn they will tend to list reasons located within the learner, or within his or her family background and culture. Rarely will they consider that at least part of the problem might lie within the teaching methods and the curriculum. Teachers tend to 'blame the victim' rather than the ways in which instruction is delivered. Some students are 'curriculum disabled' and are victimized by instruction that is ill-suited to their needs.

When teachers believe that educational failure is due to deficiencies in the learner they are likely to be pessimistic about their own ability to improve the situation. Indeed, the common response from teachers when faced with a student's learning difficulties is to lower the level of expectation and to slow the rate of teaching. The outcome from this action is that the student becomes locked in a downward spiral, where lowered expectations and a slower pace of instruction result in an increasingly significant decline in feelings of self-efficacy, together with a loss of motivation.

While factors intrinsic to the student obviously do impact upon the individual's ability to learn in school, they are all factors over which teachers have minimum control. The factors over which they have most control are those related to teaching method, curriculum content and student teacher rapport.

Reducing Educational Failure

While there are many complex factors, physical, psychological, economic and sociological, which account for each child's school performance, the basic cause of failure is the schooling process itself. Students do not enter school as failures; when students fail, it is the practices which teachers and administrators individually and collectively employ that are at fault. Unless the classroom teacher's policies and practices are viewed as the most significant conditions in determining the direction and quality of classroom learning, and unless attempts at improving classroom learning focus on the formulation of more effective teaching policies and practices, there will be no significant reduction in the educational failure of children with special needs in inclusive settings.

Classroom-based research has shown that most children with special needs can learn academic skills and attain a reasonable standard in content areas if:

- Instruction is individualised, sensitive and systematic;
- They are given constant attention, explanation, demonstration and personal help as and when they experience learning difficulties;
- They are given extra time for drill and practice;
- They are given immediate personal feedback and reinforcement and
- The learning experiences are adjusted to the level and pace of individual child.

Classroom-based research has shown that teachers who help students to be successful in basic academic skills tend to exhibit a particular set of behaviours and characteristics within their general approach to teaching. Most of the reported research presents the view that an effective teacher:

- creates a supportive learning environment,
- believes in students' ability to learn,
- believes in his or her own ability to teach,
- makes optimum use of available time through proactive planning and management,
- covers the curriculum content thoroughly, in manageable amounts, at a reasonable pace, and at a high rate of success,
- uses explicit teaching procedures such as demonstrating, modeling, explaining, questioning and giving corrective feedback,
- provides abundant opportunities for students to engage in guided and independent practice and application,

- teaches adaptively, by closely monitoring the progress of students and providing re-teaching and extra practice where necessary,
- encourages peer assistance and cooperative learning,
- revises and reviews previous learning at very regular intervals (Peter Westwood, 1998).

A number of authorities suggest that some students make much better progress in basic academic skills when they are directly and explicitly taught. In particular, slower learning students, poorly motivated students, and students from educationally disadvantaged backgrounds appear to acquire basic skills more rapidly when taught by methods involving a great deal of teacher modeling and guided practice. Direct explicit teaching emerges as one of the most convincingly successful ways of meeting the instructional needs of students with learning difficulties.

Finally, skilled teachers have something else of importance that sets them apart from less successful teachers and reduces classroom failure. That something appears to be a positive rapport with, and genuine respect for, the students they teach. Effective teachers blend their instructional skills with a more personalized and responsive approach to their students. Effective teaching combines human relationship skills, judgment, intuition, humour, knowledge of subject matter, and an understanding of different types of learning into one unified act, resulting in improved outcomes for all students.

INTERVENTIONS

In order that special needs children enrolled in schools receive quality education, stay in and complete primary education some interventions are desirable. Such interventions may be environmental, academic, social and administrative.

Environmental Intervention (Physical Settings)

Environmental intervention refers to the modifications in the physical settings of the class and school. It is an essential step for the education of special needs children in regular schools. This includes the following:

- Removal of architectural barriers like lift, ramps, furniture, etc. to facilitate easy movement of orthopaedically handicapped children, particularly the wheel-chair bound children;
- Minimizing the auditory and visual distracters in and around the classroom;
- Reducing irrelevant stimuli in the classroom;
- Arrangement for adequate illumination in the classroom;
- Proper seating arrangement;
- Sound proofing of walls and ceiling, if required;
- Carpeting the floor;
- Opaque window and
- Enclosed book cases and cup boards.

These modifications are not necessarily to be made by each and every school in our country. For example, the last four items may be applicable in schools in Western countries. Indian schools need to make the first five interventions/modifications in their classrooms.

Administrative Interventions

Administrative intervention is another important measure for implementing inclusive education. This includes the following:

- Visit of Supervising Officers/Education Officers to the schools;
- Giving feedback to teachers for increasing their efficiency;
- Financial assistance to schools for implementing inclusive education;
- Construction of resource room in schools or in the centre schools;
- Maintenance of resource room;
- Providing in-service education to teachers and the headmasters;

- Deputing teachers to visit model inclusive schools outside the state/country and
- Monitoring and evaluation of the programme.

For effective implementation of inclusive education, administrators are expected to be familiar with the concept, objectives and practices of inclusive education. Such familiarity will help the administrators in supervision, monitoring, control and for providing leadership to the headmasters of inclusive schools.

Administrators are also required to participate in awareness/ advocacy programme in inclusive education organized by the Ministry of Human Resource Development, NCERT and UNICEF.

It is evident from various literature that District Education Officers and the Block Level Education Officers rarely visit schools due to some or the other reasons. Even when they visit schools they do not give any specific feedback to teachers about what they are doing and how they are doing it. In such cases, the very purpose of supervision is lost.

Schools expect some financial assistance from the Government to meet their contingency expenditure, for purchase of aids equipments, and other instructional material, removal of architectural barriers and other environmental modifications. When such assistance is not provided by the Government other agencies such as Rotary Club, Lions Club, business houses, industries, NGOs, parent teacher associations and voluntary agencies should come forward to provide assistance in the form of finance or supply of materials to schools.

Resource room is an administrative arrangement for meeting the needs of children with disabilities. Specialized help can only be given to such children in the resource room. Thus inclusive schools should have resource room facilities. Resource rooms can be constructed either with assistance from the Government or from other agencies. Once a resource room has been constructed it must be maintained properly and used for the purpose for which it has been constructed. A teacher of the school or the inclusion facilitator should remain in charge of the resource room.

Another significant aspect of administrative intervention is that if inclusive education is to be effectively implemented then teachers should be exposed to good practices of inclusive education. They should be deputed to visit good inclusive schools either in their own state or outside the state.

Professional development of teachers and the headmaster is another aspect of administrative intervention. Teachers and headmasters might have received their professional training long back. They need to keep themselves abreast with new knowledge, skills and attitudes. Inviting teachers and headmasters to participate in workshops, organizing seminars and in-service education programmes, publication of articles on inclusive education in news papers and popular magazines and circulation of the same among schools, discussion with teachers and headmasters and clarifying their doubts about the theory and practice of inclusive education are some of the measures to be taken by administrators for professional development of teachers.

When in-service education programmes are organized for teachers they should be at least for a period of seven days and should emphasize the following aspects of inclusive education: (The list is suggestive, not prescriptive).

- Concept of inclusive education;
- Differences between inclusive education and integrated education;
- Teaching-learning strategies in inclusive education;
- Managing behaviour problems in inclusive settings;
- Making evaluation flexible;
- Curriculum adaptation;
- Strategies for developing friendships among children with special needs and other children;
- Community mobilization;

- Linkage with special schools and
- Involving parents in the education of their children.

So far as monitoring is concerned administrators may make use of the following mechanisms:

- Quarterly review;
- Seeking annual reports from the school;
- Visiting the school;
- On the sport assessment and giving suggestions. For evaluation of the programme the following strategies may be adopted:
  - Self evaluation by the headmaster;
  - Internal evaluation by the Department and
  - External evaluation by NCERT/MHRD.

Social Intervention

Involvement of the community or social intervention is a necessary condition for the success of inclusive education. The community can intervene in the programme in the following ways:

- Participating in the awareness programme;
- Participating in the decision-making process;
- Meeting the expenses of constructing the resource room;
- Sending out-of-school children to school;
- Encouraging disabled children to attend school regularly;
- Providing or helping the teacher trained in special education;
- Providing the salary of the resource teacher;
- Providing aids and equipments to the school;
- Supervising the work of teachers and giving feedback to them;
- Helping in dealing with the problems of the handicapped girl child;

- Monitoring the progress of inclusive education in the locality and
- Transforming the school into a community school.

Academic Intervention

Academic intervention is the most important intervention to ensure appropriate education for special needs children. Academic intervention consists of the following measures:

- Provision of instructional materials for children with special needs;
- Providing specialized help to children with special needs in the resource room;
- Modifying/adapting the curriculum to suit to the needs of special needs children;
- Rectifying the deficiencies of children with special needs;
- Improving the quality of teaching;
- Taking personal care of special needs children;
- Showing positive attitudes towards children with special needs;
- Adopting innovative teaching practices;
- Providing remedial instruction to children with special needs and
- Establishing linkage with special schools and utilizing the expertise and resources of special schools.

The importance of appropriate instructional materials for effective education of a child cannot be overemphasized. This is applicable in case of all learners whether they are disabled or non-disabled. Instructional materials meant for disabled children can also be used for teaching non-disabled children. Some of these materials can be procured by the schools. Teachers can also develop or improvise instructional materials for different types of disabled children.

Box 6.1: Instructional materials for children with visual impairment

Materials to be procured	*Materials to be developed*
Magnifying glass Different types of charts Embossed maps Flash cards Tape recorder Audio cassettes Models Artificial flowers	Embossed charts of different geometrical shapes Models Flowers Recorded cassettes for teaching Arithmetic, English, Science and Social Studies Large size hand-written learning materials for low-vision children

Box 6.2: Instructional materials for children with hearing impairment

Materials to be procured	*Materials to be developed*
Pictures and photographs of great men Various types of charts Speech trainer Hearing aids Overhead projector Mirror Language kits Arithmetic kits	Various kinds of pictures Colourful charts Picture albums String puppets Coloured balls Hand-drawn maps

Box 6.3: Instructional materials for children with mental retardation

Materials to be procured	*Materials to be developed*
Sensory apparatus and Montessori kits Alphabets charts Number charts Day-date calendar	Play materials and toys Materials written on a lower reading level than average Concrete objects of different sizes, shapes and colours

Instructional materials either procured or developed should be made available to all teachers of the school for teaching purposes.

One significant aspect of academic intervention is specialized help to be given to children with special needs in the resource room. Specialized help may be given by any one of the following personnel:

- Full time resource teacher of the school;
- Part-time resource teacher;

- Special school teacher;
- Special educator or
- Inclusion facilitator.

Teachers should adopt innovative practices while teaching special needs children. Participatory teaching, peer tutoring, cooperative learning, co-teaching or team teaching are some of the practices which are useful for such children.

Inclusive schools should establish linkages with the special school located in the area. The following are the ways of establishing linkages with special schools:

- Teachers consult and seek the advice of special school teachers;
- Special school teachers visit the school regularly and discuss with teachers about their problems and the solutions;
- Severely handicapped children enrolled in the school are referred to special schools for their preparation;
- Severely handicapped children who have completed their preparation in special schools are readmitted in the school;
- Instructional materials are borrowed from the special school;
- Special school teachers often teach in the inclusive school and
- Special school teachers and regular education teachers form a network of support services for children with special needs.

Creating and Maintaining Inclusive Schools

7

In chapter-3 we have discussed about what an inclusive school looks like. An inclusive school is a place where everyone belongs, is accepted, supports and is supported by his or her peers and other members of the school community. Existing school systems can not respond to the needs of children with diverse abilities. Thus there is an imperative need for reforms in the school system. All advocates for improving schools to better meet diverse students needs must join together and recognize the principle that **good schools are good schools for all students** and then act on that principle. The following elements contribute to creating and maintaining a successful inclusive school.

EVERY SCHOOL—AN INCLUSIVE SCHOOL

Inclusive education is a human right issue. Every child with special needs has a right to receive education in his neighbourhood school. In order that the right to education in the neighbourhood school is granted to every child with special needs, every primary school should be an inclusive school. In some states inclusive education is being implemented on a small scale in limited schools. Administrators should take steps for the expansion of inclusive education facilities. The social-justice approach to educational planning and management should be followed in the expansion of inclusive education. The thrust of social justice approach is: justice to all, and injustice to none.

PROVISION OF ADEQUATE STAFF

Mere expansion of inclusive education will not serve the purpose. Inclusive schools should have adequate number of regular education teachers. At present some schools have surplus teachers, and some schools have a single teacher only. The principle of rationalization of staff should be followed for providing appropriate education to all special needs children. In other words arrangement should be made in such a manner that every inclusive school should have at least five teachers. An experienced teacher of the school may be designated as inclusion facilitator and he/she should be provided training in the theory and practice of inclusive education. The inclusion facilitator can share his/ her experiences with colleagues and guide them as and when they seek such guidance.

EARLY IDENTIFICATION OF SPECIAL NEEDS CHILDREN

Special needs children should be identified as early as possible by parents in the home and later by teachers in the school. Early identification is important for the following reasons: early diagnosis of children's needs and difficulties, obtaining appropriate aids and equipments for such children, better exposure to education, better psycho-social adjustment and better achievements of special needs children.

Special needs children are usually identified by teachers based on day-to-day observation of children's progress and difficulties in school related subjects. That is all right. Reports of parents also provide useful information about their children. But teachers should not ignore reports of peers. In an ideal sense a combination of all procedures—day-to-day observation by a team of teachers, reports of parents and peers followed by use of identification tools are more reliable than any single procedure. This is not only ideal, it is also feasible.

ASSESSMENT OF SPECIAL NEEDS CHILDREN

Once special needs children are identified they must be subject to assessment—medical and psychological. Assessment is the systematic process of gathering educationally relevant information about special needs children to enable the headmaster and the teachers to make appropriate infrastructure arrangement, classroom management and to take instructional decisions.

In some cases medical assessment and psychological assessment are not possible due to unavailability of specialists in the locality and/or unwillingness of parents to take their children to district hospital for assessment purpose. In such cases teachers can rely on scientific/formal functional assessment procedures. Functional assessment can provide authentic information about the child's strength and weaknesses.

At present no specific direction is available from the State Governments about the specialists who will conduct medical and psychological assessment of learning disabled children as a result of which these children remain unassessed in inclusive schools. Under this situation it is better to have functional assessment of LD children done than to have no assessment at all. Regular teachers can conduct functional assessment of special needs children.

ESTABLISHING A SCHOOL PHILOSOPHY

An important strategy for creating a quality inclusive school is to establish a school philosophy based on the democratic, egalitarian principles of inclusion, belonging, and provision of quality education to all children. A quality inclusive system to education by its very nature focuses on the needs of the 'whole child', not merely on academic achievement. If schools are to focus on the development of the 'whole child', their underlying philosophy needs to be that the education they provide will be relevant for each child at least in three spheres: the academic, the social and emotional, and personal and collective responsibility and citizenship.

Inclusive schools in different countries maintain a philosophy such as the following:

- Every child belongs to the school;
- Every child is welcome to the school;
- Quality education should be provided to children with special needs;

- Children with special needs are accepted as equal members of the school community;
- Every child can learn;
- Children with special needs should be educated in regular classrooms/schools;
- No child should be denied admission on the ground of disability;
- Education of special needs children is the responsibility of each and every teacher; and
- The school should be a supportive community.

It is very often found that although inclusive schools maintain a certain philosophy which is a mission statement, such mission statement in most schools is formulated by the headmaster and the teachers. All others who are directly related with the education of children—parents, community members and student representatives should also be involved in the decision-making and formulation of the mission statement. This will ensure their active participation and co-operation in making the school a community where everyone belongs, is accepted and respected, and is supported by others.

ENROLMENT DRIVE AND MEASURES FOR RETENTION

Enrolment drive through parent contact programme and community awareness programme can help to increase enrolment of special needs children, particularly girls and in rural areas. Measures should also be taken so that all special needs children enrolled in schools stay in and complete primary education. Some of the measures to be taken by the school, teachers and administrators are: (i) Teachers must appropriately be trained to provide education that is relevant for the life and needs of special needs education, particularly girls, so that they develop interest and motivation for the learning tasks, (ii) Teaching-learning practices such as peer tutoring, co-operative learning and individualized instruction should be adopted by teachers, (iii) Teasing and bullying by peers should be discouraged in the school, (iv) Appropriate instructional and learning materials should be developed by teachers or procured by the school which will make their learning meaningful, (v) Children with and without disabilities should be encouraged and guided to develop friendships which will reduce peer rejection, (vi) Parents should be advised and educated to take personal care of their special needs children on matters relating to regular attendance in the school, giving support for doing home assignments and making satisfactory progress in the school. Research by Fuller, et al. (1999) has demonstrated that to achieve academically children must attend school regularly. A study of village-based schools in Malawi found that students with higher rates of attendance had greater learning gains, and lower rates of repetition, a finding consistent with many other studies (Miske, D., et al., 1998).

PROVISION OF INCENTIVES

Incentives in the form of stipends, scholarships and financial assistance should be provided by the Government and/or other bodies/organizations so as to increase their attendance in the school and reduce drop out rate.

REMOVAL OF ARCHITECTURAL BARRIERS

It is also found that a large number of orthopaedically handicapped children are now attending regular schools. In order that such children, particularly the wheel-chair bound children, do not face any difficulty in attending school and for their movements, architectural barriers should be removed in the school.

HETEROGENEOUS GROUPING

Inclusive schools in different countries differ with regard to placement of children with special needs after they are identified. In some schools special needs children are directly integrated in the heterogeneous setting of the regular classroom. But in some other schools special needs children are placed part-time in the heterogeneous setting of the regular classroom and part-time in the homogenous group in the resource room.

Educating all children in the inclusive setting essentially means the heterogeneous grouping of children in the same regular classes and school activities. Although there are advantages of heterogeneous grouping such as allowing for shared responsibility among children, learning from modeling, learning from and helping each other, better understanding among children with and without special needs, ensuring friendships among children, and offsetting the potential stereotyping and/or stigmatization, some students may need to be homogenously grouped occasionally for instruction in the resource room. For example, the blind child may need instruction in Braille, orientation and mobility training. The hearing impaired children may need instruction in sign language, and speech reading. The mentally retarded child may need instruction in daily living skills, or the speech handicapped child may need training in communication skills. For all such training, homogenous grouping in the resource room is desired. But such homogenous grouping should be of short duration as far as possible. If limited grouping is necessary, children should be grouped according to their specific instructional needs and for not more than a couple of subject areas and one or two periods. Thus, they should be allowed to spend the majority of the school day in heterogeneous groupings.

PROVISION OF FACILITIES, AIDS AND EQUIPMENTS

Mere opening of a new inclusive school or re-designating an existing primary school as inclusive school will not serve the purpose. In order to ensure quality education for special needs children, inclusive schools should be provided with facilities, appropriate aids and equipments. Research has demonstrated that the quality of school facilities seems to have an indirect effect on learning. A study by Carron and Chau (1996) found a strong correlation between school facilities and pupils' achievement. Studies by Willms (2000) also found similar correlation between school facilities and low test scores and higher grade repetition.

It is also found that primary schools in our country are not well-equipped with facilities due to lack of government assistance. Hence, the schools should mobilize the community, and may approach business houses, Lions Club, Rotary Club and similar organizations for providing required facilities for children with special needs.

AVOIDING PSYCHOLOGICAL SEPARATION

Even when every child is placed in the mainstream, separation still occurs on a psychological level in the minds of children, teachers and parents. This psychological separation should be avoided. All children should be viewed simply as children, each with his/her own unique characteristics, rather than viewing some with "special needs."

Similarly, all educators/teachers should be referred to as regular educators or just simply educators rather than some being "special educators." To accomplish this, special educators can become educators with expertise in Braille, speech reading, behaviour modification, etc. There should be more integration of personnel and resources than just physical proximity. Integration on a psychological level in the minds of everyone is also important to achieve a sense of oneness or community where everyone belongs, where everyone supports and is supported by others, and is a natural and integral part of the mainstream.

PROFESSIONAL DEVELOPMENT OF TEACHERS

Professional development can help overcome shortcomings that may have been part of teachers' pre-service education and keep teachers abreast with new knowledge, and practices in the field of inclusive education. Professional development of teachers has a direct impact on student's achievement.

At present the steps taken by the administrators for professional development of teachers are not adequate. Effective professional development may take many forms—formal off-site kinds of programmes, dialogues, reflective interactions with colleagues, workshops, peers' and supervisors' observations, reading journals, etc. (UNICEF, 2000).

Anderson (2000) found that teachers supported with in-service as well as external workshop training improved significantly in their abilities to use child-centred teaching and learning behaviour. In India, an effective programme used interactive video technology to reach a large number of teachers who sought professional development. This programme found that training using interactive video technology led to improved conceptual understanding of pedagogical issues for a large number of geographically dispersed teachers (Maheswari and Raina, 1998).

CHANGING HEARTS AND MINDS

What is important is teachers' commitment, competence and creativity which continues to be central to the success of children with special needs. The urgent task is to change hearts and minds of teachers, encouraging their openness to the values, aims and strategies of inclusive education and their commitment to the human right of all children. NGOs and people having knowledge, skills and attitudes need to share their knowledge and experience with those just starting out.

ACCOUNTABILITY OF TEACHERS

Our experience with the Centrally Sponsored Scheme of IEDC shows that education of children with disabilities in regular schools was considered to be a single teacher's responsibility. The resource teacher was accountable for the success or failure of education of children with disabilities. If the school did not have a resource teacher, education of children with disabilities was no body's responsibility. This resulted in poor academic performance and increasing rate of dropout of such children. If inclusion is to be successful every teacher including the headmaster should be accountable for increasing enrolment and retention, providing quality education to such children, creating a supportive learning environment in the class, ensuring acceptance and respect for such children and building friendship and solidarity among children with and without special needs.

DEVELOPING FRIENDSHIP

School personnel have not always recognized that, in order to educate the whole child, they must attend to students' needs for acceptance, belonging, and friends. School is the place where young children spend a substantial amount of time and where many of their social connections are made. Furthermore, friendships and relationships are actually preconditions to learning in schools (Forest, 1990). If a student feels unconnected and if he or she does not belong, then the student is not able to learn to his or her fullest potential. Therefore, people working in schools must share with parents the responsibility for helping students make positive connections with each other in their schools and neighbourhood communities. Educators and families have found that intentional, deliberate efforts often must be made in order to create and support opportunities for friendships to develop in school that carry over to after school social opportunities for students. Some strategies that can be used to develop friendships have been cited by Stainback and Stainback (1996) as follows:

- Promoting cooperative rather than competitive goal structures in the classroom and school;
- Establishing classroom and school rituals or traditions in which everyone is provided the support necessary in order to participate equally and fully;
- Finding opportunities throughout the school day to present students perceived as different in a positive way to their peers;
- Ensuring that in every classroom and school activity accommodations are made so that everyone, including students with challenging needs, can participate actively;
- Infusing positive values of respect, appreciation of people who are different, and cooperation into the curriculum itself; and
- Involving students in decision-making regarding classroom and school policies for supporting each other in school.

In addition to these strategies cocurricular activities should be organized in schools in such a manner that children with and without disabilities can participate together. Schools clearly must become caring communities where all students feel valued, safe, connected and cared for.

POSITIVE ATTITUDES OF TEACHERS

A large number of teachers do not show positive attitudes towards special needs children. Such children are also not accepted by these teachers. As Kenneth Eklindh of UNESCO section for inclusive education says "Negative attitudes are the main obstacle to schooling children with disabilities" (*Education Today*, No. 7, October-December 2003, p. 8). Some teachers believe that there are already too many problems educating 'normal children.' Including special needs children in the regular class creates additional problems. Inclusion is about valuing diversity. "Diversity among children is to be viewed as a gift, not a problem for teachers" (The 46th Session of UNESCO's International Conference in Education, Geneva, 5-8 September 2001).

ENSURING QUALITY EDUCATION

Inclusion should not mean dumping children into the regular education classes. Teachers have to ensure quality education for all. Quality education does not simply include cognitive learning. Human values, attitudes, skills and competencies are also important. Guaranteeing and respecting the right to education in the neighbourhood school is a challenge which every teacher has to meet with dedication and sincerity otherwise inclusion will be a frustrated attempt, if not a disaster.

INCLUSION AS AN INTEGRAL PART OF DUTY

Most teachers demand extra allowance because they believe inclusive education is an extra work and thus extra allowance should be paid for extra work. This is not what the teachers in Indian schools believe, most teachers of other countries may have similar beliefs. Even a Namibian case study (2001) found that teachers still think inclusion means extra work and should be an extra-mural activity. Teachers need to be convinced that like any other activity inclusion of special needs children in the regular classes should be considered as an integral part of their work. This calls for specific instruction from the Government in this regard.

EARLY CHILDHOOD EDUCATION AND CARE

A large study in 12 Latin American Countries found that attendance at ECEC centers coupled with higher levels of parental involvement which includes parents reading to young children is associated with higher test scores and lower rates of grade repetition in primary schools (Willms, 2000). This finding implies that intervention in the form of provision for early childhood education and care for special needs children can ensure their better performance in primary schools.

ADAPTING THE CURRICULUM

In order to meet the special educational needs of children in inclusive settings, teachers have to adapt the curriculum in terms of contents, methods of teaching, evaluation procedures, time, level of support, rules and regulations. This has two implications: (i) Teachers must be trained properly on how to adapt the curriculum, and (ii) They must be granted autonomy to do so, otherwise it may create administrative problems.

ENCOURAGING PARTICIPATORY LEARNING

A large number of teachers report that special needs children are not capable of learning the basic academic skills in inclusive education settings. But a number of educators have demonstrated that children with diverse educational needs can participate and learn in meaningful ways in regular education classes, and this is desirable also. For example, during map reading activity in environmental studies, the orthopaedically impaired child may be called upon to discuss the agricultural production of a particular district, the mildly hearing impaired child may be required to identify colour used in the map to indicate the specific agricultural production of the district, while the learning disabled child may be requested to hold a corner of the map. Similarly, in the reading class the learning disabled child may be required to read out loud, the visually impaired child may be requested to listen to the story and answer questions, while the mentally challenged child may pick out pictures that describe the story. A non-disabled child may provide support to the mentally challenged child to pick out the right pictures. Thus, in inclusive, heterogeneous classrooms, children with special needs should be encouraged to participate in activities depending upon what they need to learn and what they are capable of doing, but with flexibility. If appropriately organized, regular education classes can provide a variety of learning activities and challenges for children with a range of learning needs, interests, and capabilities.

MAKING THE MAINSTREAM SENSITIVE AND ADAPTIVE

It is also observed that regular teachers find fault with special needs children for their failure in schools. If a child fails to be successful in academic subjects whose fault is it? If a child fails in the school and then fails in life, the school cannot sit back and blame the child. We have to describe it as a failure not by the child but by the schools. This, of course, will require the identification of appropriate and challenging goals for each child in the mainstream rather than requiring them to learn exactly the same thing or always be at the same level of proficiency. It will also be necessary to provide support and assistance to children when necessary.

Growing number of parents and educators are now convinced that it can be done, given that the mainstream is sensitive to individual differences, and teachers and children are provided adequate support and assistance. The reason is that, if it is beginning to be done successfully in some schools in the US, Canada, Italy, Australia, and a number of other countries, then there is no reason why it will not be successfully done in our country. However, it will be difficult to achieve widespread success if the school is unwilling to provide each child the support necessary for him or her to be in the mainstream, and adapt and adjust, when necessary, the mainstream to accommodate all children. Thus, the key is the willingness to visualize, work for, and achieve a mainstream that is adaptive and supportive of everyone.

Segregation has been on the march for at least a century. Now in some States of our country, integrated education has been in operation for quite a long time. Even, at present, many schools do not know how to adapt and modify the curriculum to meet diverse needs of children, deal with their behaviour problems and to provide the tools, techniques and supports some children need to be successful in the mainstream. Thus, achieving full inclusion of all children is likely to be a challenging undertaking. However, the goals of having inclusive schools where everyone belongs, has friends and support is far too important than not to accept the challenge.

MAKING THE SCHOOL EFFECTIVE

There are a number of critical elements for enhancing the efficiency of teachers and the effectiveness of inclusive schools. It is noteworthy to mention here the views of some experts in the field.

Stainback and Stainback (1990) have suggested the following practical strategies for making inclusive schools effective:

1. Establish a school philosophy.
2. Follow the principle of natural proportions for enrolling special needs children.
3. Include individuals (students with disabilities, parents, non-disabled students and teachers) in any discussion and planning for inclusion).
4. Develop networks of support for teachers and students.
5. Integrate students, personnel and resources.
6. Adapt the curriculum.
7. Maintain flexibility.

Schaffner and Buswell (1991) have suggested four additional strategies for making inclusive schools effective:

1. Provide strong leadership.
2. Promote school wide and classroom cultures that welcome, appreciate, and accommodate diversity.
3. Use deliberate processes to ensure accountability.
4. Celebrate successes and learn from challenges.

ENHANCING THE EFFICIENCY OF TEACHERS

In order to enhance the efficiency of teachers Karagiannis and his associates (1994) have suggested three interdependent practical components—the organizational component, the procedural component and the instructional component. The organizational component includes support networking which involves the co-ordination of teams and individuals who support each other by formal and informal connections. The procedural component includes collaboration and consultation which involve individuals with a variety of expertise who work together to plan and implement programmes for diverse students in mainstream environments. The instructional components include co-operative learning, peer tutoring, heterogeneous grouping and learning groups for instructional and recreational activities in which students of varying abilities and interests can achieve their potential.

The proposal contained in the National Curriculum Framework for School Education (NCERT, 2000) for promoting inclusive education in our country is also noteworthy. It states:

"Definite action at the level of curriculum makers, teachers, writers of teaching-learning materials and evaluation experts is required for the success of this strategy. This has to include:

- developing appropriate supplementary instructional material for learners with special needs;
- making appropriate modifications in the contents, its presentation and transaction strategies to facilitate conceptual clarity among learners with different special needs;
- developing and working out appropriate learner friendly evaluation procedures for learners with different special needs;
- preparing teachers with initial induction and sensitizing them through in-service education programmes to help them attend to the special needs of the learners with various challenges and equipping these teachers

with skills, competencies and strategies required to cater to the diversity in an inclusive setting;

- developing comprehensive guidelines for teachers to define educational goals for all learners in the inclusive settings and
- mobilizing community resources for support to learners with special needs. These could be in the form of resource centers."

The above discussion is not exhaustive. There may be other elements which contribute to creating and maintaining an inclusive school. To begin with, we should not be overambitious for achieving full inclusion too soon. We need to move slowly but steadily, from strength to strength, our motto being:

Good, Better, Best
We Will Not Take Rest;
Until Good Becomes Better
And Better Becomes Best.

Review of Selected Studies

8

The review of related literature is of paramount importance for the researcher. An investigator must be aware of the new researches conducted in the field of study in the past and only then he is in a position to contribute something in original. It is through the review of related studies that the researcher knows the work that have already been done over a period of time. He knows the areas untouched or unexplored and has an idea of the scope of the subject or the study in all aspects. Without a critical study of the related literature, the investigator will be groping in the dark and perhaps uselessly, repeat the work already done. Therefore, to save time, energy, and resources, it is necessary to undertake a detailed and penetrating study of all available literature.

Review of related literature serves as a guide post not only with regard to the quantum of work done in the field but also enables us to perceive the gap and lacuna in the concerned field of research. The investigator's analysis and review of such resourceful studies work as an impetus which pushes the investigator into greater details and wider applicability of the problems in hand to provide new ideas, theories, explanations or hypothesis.

"The orientation provided by survey of related literature is helpful in making a straight forward statement of need for the investigation. The review of related literature promotes a greater understanding of the problem and its crucial aspects and ensures the avoidance of unnecessary duplication. For conducting research in any field, the research worker is required to have full acquaintance with the library and its many sources to take advantage of studies undertaken earlier.

Every research project should be based on relevant thinking and proper plan and procedure. When a new research is not based on relevant thinking and proper plan and procedure, when a new research is not based on a thorough review of literature, it becomes an isolated entity, bearing at best accidental relevance to what has been done before. The findings of earlier experiments encourage the new worker to give importance to useful projects in education, and the research worker is able to avoid the past mistakes or defects in the procedure.

The main findings of some selected studies conducted abroad are cited here:

Eckman (1993) studied the attitudes of educators towards the inclusion of children with moderate or severe handicaps in regular education classroom. The study was directed at describing attitudes towards inclusion and at eliciting reasons why attitudes are what they are. The objective was to see if attitudes of educators in sites that have been operating for several years are different from attitudes of educators in sites that are newer. The data were collected from thirty schools across Pennsylvania and provided 543 individual responses. Two factors ANOVA showed significant differences in acceptance between elementary and secondary respondents. Elementary respondents were more accepting of inclusion. There were indicators that educators feel that the level of inclusion operating in their school is the best level regardless of whether that is 100% inclusion or mostly special education placement. Those in favour of inclusion had wider attitudes of acceptance.

Pickett (1993) examined the relationship between school structure and culture and students' views of diversity and inclusive education. The populations studied were from schools in two separate districts: one identified as consciously advocating for the principles of inclusion and the other with traditional approaches to education. Data were gathered through focus groups of seventh and eighth grade students, depth interviews with faculty, and document review. Significant structural and cultural differences were found between the two schools. Additionally, students in both schools conceptualized differences in dissimilar ways, and their views of inclusive education differed drastically. Students in the traditional school characterized the possibility of inclusion as a potential "disaster" and unanimously believed that it was a bad idea. In contrast, the students in the inclusive school revealed a broader, most positive concept of diversity, subsuming differences in a more accepting frame of "Like us." Despite the noted imperfections, these students also characterized inclusion as worthy and workable, with benefit to all students. A key finding is that, despite previous school experiences, all students strongly believed in the importance of belonging and the worthiness of supporting their peers.

Devis (1994) conducted a study on how administrators and teachers feel about full inclusion of students with moderate to severe disabilities. The philosophy of educating students with moderate to severe disabilities in neighbourhood schools and even in the regular classrooms has increasingly become recognized nationally as the "best educational practice." Being able to attend neighbourhood/home schools allows these students to participate meaningfully in school situations with "normal" peers, just as they hopefully would in their neighbourhoods. The term for this "practice" or "service delivery model" is called full inclusion. This study examined the views of regular and special education teachers and administrators on what is critical to ensure the success of full inclusion of students with moderate to severe disabilities in home/neighbourhood schools and also to determine their attitude towards the inclusion of these students in home schools.

Galis (1994) conducted a study on attitudes and beliefs of special and regular educators in the State of Georgia. The purpose of this study was to investigate the perceptions and beliefs of regular and special education administrators and teachers in the State of Georgia regarding the provision of services to students, including at-risk students and students with disabilities. The study investigated school reform issues that revolve around the concept of inclusive education. It was found that most responders strongly agreed that it is important to make modifications for students who need adaptations to benefit from a particular instructional environment. The responders also believed that special education provides a valuable service for students with disabilities. It is important for student's progress to be graded according to ability rather than only with standardized measures according to the sample that responded to this survey. They further opined that maximum class size should be reduced when students with disabilities are placed in regular classrooms.

Yeager (1994) made analysis of absenteeism, achievement and self-concept of elementary students in an inclusive classroom. The study's results confirmed that inclusive model for special education services was effective in the interaction of the positive self-concept with good attendance and produced similar results on students' achievement. Although students with disabilities compared to their peers have enduring significant differences in the achievement levels tested, Class-Within-A-Class results presented a positive academic self-concept, and academic progress for all students involved.

Afzali (1995) reviewed literature on inclusion of deaf students in the regular classroom and perceptions of regular educators and deaf educators relating to inclusive education. Many educators believe that all students benefit when students with special needs are taught in regular classes. Recent data indicate that three-fourths of the hearing impaired students' population is served, at least part time, in regular classroom settings. But this practice is controversial. Many deaf educators and parents of deaf children believe that the purpose of educating these students is to teach them to function in a non-hearing society. This study assessed perceptions of teachers about the full inclusion of deaf/hard-of-hearing students in the regular classroom. Views regarding outcomes of inclusive education and the desirability of various educational conditions were related to the respondent's position and experience.

Doyle (1995) made a qualitative inquiry into the roles and responsibilities of para-educators who support students with severe disabilities in inclusive classrooms. The purpose of this research was to gain an initial understanding of (a) the roles and responsibilities of para-educators, and (b) the interaction patterns among members of the instructional triad (i.e., para-educator, general educator and special educator). Findings indicate that there was a great deal of variability associated with what it means to be a highly effective para-educator. These specific variables were identified as being related to para-educator's "effectiveness." These variables are: affective characteristics of para-educators' attitudes toward students, para-educator's support to the general and special educators in fulfilling their teaching responsibilities. In addition, five factors emerged that appear to contribute to understanding the variety of roles and responsibilities of highly effective para-educators. These factors are: (a) pattern of interaction among triad members, (b) para-educators' skills and training, (c) specific student characteristics, (d) classroom structure, and (e) experience of the general and special educators.

Herman (1995) examined the perceptions of elementary school principals regarding the desirability and feasibility of adapting regular elementary classrooms and programmes for the inclusion of children with moderate and severe disabilities. Responding elementary principals in this study identified 95% of the presented adaptations as significantly more desirable than feasible with demographic factors having little or no effect. Moderate to high scores on the feasibility scale, however, indicated that principals do not view implementation of the adaptations as impractical. Conclusions of the study emphasized that the differing views of desirability and feasibility may be attributed to either a perceived lack of available resources or administrative autonomy or both.

Quality indicators in inclusive education programmes were studied by Gorne (1997). This study examined the relationship that exists between regular education teachers' degree of satisfaction with including students with disabilities in their classroom demonstrated in the programme. The results indicated that the teachers were successfully implementing programme quality indicators in the areas of classroom organization, instructional methods, staff collaboration and support, and student social support. There appeared to be a positive significant relationship between use of these indicators and teacher's satisfaction with their experience of including students with disabilities in their classrooms. Teachers were also concerned regarding professional preparation, training and support.

A study by Barrafato (1998) examined the extent to which supports such as school funds and resources, parental and teacher attitude, in-service training, and planning contribute to the successful inclusion of children with disabilities at the early childhood level. Results demonstrated that overall the children were socially integrated and adjusted to their settings. All teachers and parents identified certain factors which must be in place to successfully integrate children in regular classrooms. The importance of a teacher's aid, increased support services, appropriate in-serving training for teachers and smaller class sizes were stressed.

Brown (1998) conducted a study on Middle School personnel's attitudes towards inclusive education in a suburban Texas school district. The purpose of the study was to examine the criterion variable of school personnel's attitude towards inclusive education and how they are related to the variables of academic assignment, gender, inclusive education experience, and the number of years of experience in education. Results revealed that there was a significant difference between the academic assignment groups on the criterion variable of attitude towards inclusive education. The analysis of data supported a significant difference between the teachers', counselors' and administrators' attitudes towards inclusion. The findings in this study support that administrators demonstrated a more positive attitude towards inclusion than teachers and counsellors. There was also a significant relationship between attitude towards inclusive education and the composite set of variables: academic assignment, gender, inclusive education experience, and number of years in education. However, there was a significant independent relationship between attitude towards inclusive education and the predictor variable of academic assignment. Interaction was found between inclusive education experience and gender on the criterion variable of attitude towards inclusive education.

Horton (1998) investigated the opinions of parents of both disabled and non-disabled elementary children regarding inclusion of disabled students in regular education classes. Results indicated that parents with disabled children had more favourable opinions about inclusion than did those with non-disabled children. Parents with disabled children were more accepting of inclusion than were those with non-disabled children in inclusive settings. Parents' answers differed depending on the type of disability being included. Regardless of their child's disability or inclusion status, the ranking of disability types from most acceptable for inclusion to least acceptable were: social, sensory, motor, academic and behavioural.

Mendez (1998) conducted a study to investigate the effect of teachers' perceived role stress, perceived self-efficacy, and support for research based effective teaching behaviours on their attitudes towards inclusive education. The results of the study indicated that support for research based effective teaching behaviours not only had an indirect effect through role stress, but also had the most direct effect on teachers' attitudes towards inclusive education. Teachers' efficacy beliefs did not contribute to the hypothesized models.

The inclusion of students with special needs in regular education classrooms has become a major focus of current educational reform, and regular education classroom teachers will play a significant role in the educational experiences of children with special needs who are included in the regular education classrooms. Given that a relationship exists between attitudes and behaviour, the attitudes of teachers towards inclusion related issues will play a significant role in their interactions with children with special needs and hence, influence the quality of these students' experience.

In a study by Treder (1998) entitled "Teacher effectiveness and teacher attitudes towards children with special needs—implications for inclusive education," the attitudes of effective and typical teachers towards inclusion-related issues were compared. The results of the study indicated (a) adaptive and appropriate student behaviours deemed to be critical to a successful adjustment in their classrooms, and (b) inappropriate and maladaptive student behaviours were deemed to be unacceptable in their classrooms. The study also found that more effective teachers indicated greater interaction with special needs students and indicated higher levels of promotion of inclusive practices in their schools.

Zahn (1998) investigated the perceptions and attitudes of elementary school teachers towards the practice of inclusion, its implementation, impact and future. The study revealed that although the majority of teachers indicated support for the philosophy of inclusion, many teachers do not seem to believe it can work within the parameters of their school setting. Pre-service and in-service training teachers do seem to be addressing the instructional needs of teachers working within inclusive classrooms. However, teachers still feel that the training they are receiving is not extensive enough to meet their needs. Whatever may be the attitude towards disabilities or the practice of inclusion, it is clear that teachers need support, both through local and State administrative practices and staff development.

Clasberry (2000) conducted a study on perceptions of inclusive education held by general education teachers at different grade levels. Results indicated that general education teachers generally felt insufficiently prepared for students with disabilities. Significant relationships existed among teachers at different grade levels and with different years of teaching experiences.

Hill (2000) conducted a study on the relationship between teacher beliefs and inclusive education. Findings of the study revealed that teaching efficacy was negatively correlated with the perceived level of support needed to make curricular modifications. Second, years of experience were negatively correlated with the perceived level of support needed for instruction.

Naidu (2000) studied Head Start teachers' conceptions of full inclusion of young children. This study examined the conceptions that four teachers in a Midwest Urban Head Start programme held about inclusion. Findings indicated that teachers (a) viewed inclusion of all students as a moral imperative, (b) believed that inclusive education meant that all children were teachable, and (c) expressed the own sense of self-efficacy and worth, which included their positive effect on all children and their roles as social change agents.

O'Reilly (2000) made a longitudinal study of student placement and persistence in inclusive settings. The researcher used both qualitative and quantitative research methods to investigate whether and when students with disabilities are placed in inclusive settings, how long students persist in inclusive settings, and whether selected student and district characteristics influence placement and persistence. The findings of the study revealed that although many students with disabilities are initially placed in regular education classes for receiving special education services, most students do not persist in those settings. Inclusion is not really happening in those settings, as the environment is more restrictive. Students with non-cognitive disabilities are most likely to be placed in and persist in inclusive settings. Both students requiring academic intervention and students needing environmental adaptions are similarly unlikely to persist.

A study on teacher perceptions regarding new knowledge needed for inclusion of children with severe multiple disabilities was conducted by Ricciato (2000). The study found that the professional development needs of the regular and special education teachers were not significantly different. It also affirmed that the perceived training needs of the teachers are congruent with promising practices identified in the literature. Many teachers had participated in professional development programmes which were considered as essential in order to move forward with inclusion initiatives. While 93% of the teachers either agreed or strongly agreed that inclusion is a positive concept, their level of agreement on including children with disabilities decreased commensurately with the severity of the disabilities. While teachers agree on inclusion philosophy they are concerned with the functional aspects of inclusion which must be examined closely.

Wills (2000) carried out a study on the effects of government restructuring on inclusive education – perceptions of educators in a school division in Alberta. Four major findings emerged from this study. First, inclusive education is being constrained by government restructuring to the point where serious consideration is being given to abandoning inclusive education in favour of a more cost-effective segregated model of special education programme. Second aspects of restructuring involving shared decision-making and the devolution of authority to the school site facilitated inclusive education. Third, aspects of restructuring that constrained inclusive education included (a) the philosophical underpinnings of a business model that are incongruent with the philosophy of inclusion, (b) the emphasis on fiscal restraint and (c) complete decentralization of responsibility for special education to the school site. Fourth, educators identified specific strategies for how effective inclusion could occur within the parameters of restructuring.

Maricle (2001) conducted a study on attitudes of New Jersey public secondary school principals towards inclusive education and educational strategies related to its practice. Principals appeared to have positive attitudes towards the inclusion of students with disabilities in all categories surveyed, with the exception of students with the most severe disabilities. Finally, all three educational strategies (in-class support, use of an instructional assistant, and curriculum adaptations) were viewed as effective strategies for inclusion. Principals, in general, supported inclusion of students with disabilities in their schools.

This overview of studies conducted abroad reveals that most of the studies have focused on attitudes of regular teachers, special education teachers, para-educators and principals towards inclusive education. Few studies have been also conducted on perception and beliefs of principals and administrators about the desirability and feasibility of inclusive education at primary level. Another trend has been to study the roles and responsibilities of para-educators. Training needs of teachers, teacher effectiveness, student placement and persistence, opinion of parents of children with and without disabilities about inclusive education were also subject of interest for the researchers.

Studies conducted abroad leave a gap which needs to be filled in. It is not enough to study the attitudes of regular education teachers, special education teachers, principals and administrators towards inclusive education. Beliefs and opinions of parents and administrators are important but that is not the end of the story. We have to ensure that the programmes and practices of inclusive education are appropriate for the particular stage of education and types of children with special needs enrolled in schools.

Bibliography

Afzali, E. (1995). Inclusion of deaf students in the regular classroom: Perceptions of regular educators and deaf educators. *Dissertation Abstracts International,* Vol. 56, No. 6, p. 2195A.

Ainscow, M., Howes, A., Farrell, P. and Frankha. J. (2003). Making sense of the development of inclusive practices. *European Journal of Special Needs Education,* Vol. 18, No. 2, pp. 227-242.

Anderson, F. (2000). Ongoing professional development of teachers. *Defining Quality in Education.* Paris, UNICEF.

Ashman, A. and Elkins, J. (eds.) (1998). *Educating Children with Special Needs* (3rd ed.). Sydney, Prentice Hall.

Azad, Y.A. (1996). Integration of disabled in common schools. *A Survey Study of IEDC in the Country.* New Delhi, NCERT.

Ballard, K. (1995). Inclusion in practice: A case study of Meta theory and action. Paper delivered at the symposium on inclusion and exclusion. University of Cambridge.

Bartons, L. (ed.) (1998). *The Politics of Special Educational Needs.* Lewes, Falmer Press.

Bauwens, J. and Hourcade, J.J. (1995). *Cooperative Teaching: Rebuilding the School House for All Students.* Austin, TX.

Bayers, R. (2001). Working towards inclusion. *British Journal of Special Education,* Vol. 28, No. 4, pp. 158-159.

Bearne, E. (ed.) (1996). *Differentiation and Diversity in the Primary School.* London, Routledge.

Belmont, B. and Verillon, A. (1999). Integration of disabled children in French schools: Partnership between mainstream school teachers and special professions. *European Journal of Special Needs Education,* Vol. 14, No. 1, pp. 1-11.

Booth, T. (1999). Inclusion and exclusion in policy in England: Who contracts the agenda. In F. Armstrong, D. Armstrong and L. Barton (eds.) *Inclusive Education Policy, Contexts and Comparative Perspectives.* London, Fulton.

Cambra, C. and Silvestre, N. (2003). Students with special educational needs in the inclusive classroom: Social integration and self-concept. *European Journal of Special Needs Education,* Vol. 18, No. 2, pp. 197-208.

Carpenter, S.L. and King-Sears, M. (1997). Strategy instruction. In D. Bradley, M. King-Sears and D. Tessier–Switlick (eds.) *Teaching Students in Inclusive Settings.* Boston, Allyn & Bacon.

Carron, L. and Chau, M. (1996). Quality of school facilities and its effect on learning. *Defining Quality in Education.* Paris, UNICEF.

Chaves, I.M. (1997). Historical overview of special education in the United States. In P. Bates et al. (eds.) *Mainstreaming: Problems, Potentials and Perspectives,* Minneapolis, National Support Systems Project.

Clasberry, G.A. (2000). Perceptions of inclusive education held by general education teachers at different grade levels. *Dissertation Abstracts International,* Vol. 61, No. 9, p. 3512.

Clough, P. and Carbett, J. (2000). *Theories of Inclusive Education: A Students' Guide.* London, Paul Chapman Publishing Ltd.

Cole, P. and Chan, L. (1990). *Methods and Strategies for Special Education.* Melbourne, Prentice Hall.

Conway, R. (1996). Curriculum adaptations. In P. Foreman (ed.) *Integration and Inclusion in Action.* Sydney, Harcourt, Brace.

Cramer, S. (1998). *Collaboration: A Successful Strategy for Special Education.* Boston, Allyn & Bacon.

Cullinan, D., Sabornie, E.J., and Crossland, C.L. (1992). Social mainstreaming of mildly handicapped students.

The Elementary School Journal, Vol. 92, No. 3, pp. 339-351.

Dash, M. (2001). Classroom for All. *In Orientation Package for Teacher Educators.* New Delhi, NCERT.

Dash, M. (2005). *Education of Exceptional Children*, New Delhi, Atlantic Publishers and Distributors (P) Ltd.

Dash, M. (2005). Innovative practices in inclusive settings. Paper presented in the National Conference on EFA, Bareilly.

Dash, M. and Dash, N. (2005). *Fundamentals of Educational Psychology*, New Delhi, Atlantic Publishers and Distributors (P) Ltd.

Dash, M. and Dash, N. (2005). *Essentials of Exceptionality and Special Education,* New Delhi, Atlantic Publishers and Distributors (P) Ltd.

Dash, N. (2005). Reducing educational failure in inclusive settings. Paper presented in the National Conference on EFA, Bareilly.

Davis, S.W. (1994). Full inclusion of students with moderate to severe disabilities: How do administrators and teachers feel about it? *Dissertations Abstract International,* Vol. 55, No. 7, January (1995), p. 1905A.

Doyle, H.B. (1995). A qualitative inquiry into the roles and responsibilities of para-educators who support students with severe disabilities in inclusive classrooms. *Dissertation Abstracts International,* Vol. 56, No. 6, p. 2198A.

Dayson, A. (2001). Special needs in the twenty-first century: Where we have been and where we are going. *British Journal of Special Education,* Vol. 28, No. 1, pp. 24-29.

Eckman, R.E. (1993). Attitudes of educators in GATEWAYS sites toward the inclusion of children with moderate or severe handicaps in regular education classrooms. *Dissertation Abstracts International,* Vol. 54, No. 5, p. 1756A.

Evans, J. and Lunt, I. (2002). Inclusive education: Are there limits. *European Journal of Special Needs Education,* Vol. 17, No. 1.

Ferguson, P. and Asch, A. (1989). Lessons from life: Personal and parental perspectives on school, childhood, and disability. In D. Biklen, A. Ford and D. Ferguson (eds.) *Disability and Society*. Chicago, National Society for the Study of Education, pp. 108-140.

Fernandez, G., Koenig, C., Mani, M.N.G. and Tensi, S. (1999). *See with the Blind*. Bangalore, Books for Change and CBM International.

Frolin, C. (2001). Inclusion: Identifying potential stressors for regular class teachers. *Educational Research*, Vol. 43, No. 3, pp. 235-245.

Fuller, S. and et al. (1999). Academic achievement and school attendance. *Defining Quality in Education*. Paris, UNICEF.

Galis, S.A. (1994). Inclusive education: Attitudes and beliefs of special and regular educators in the State of Georgia. *Dissertation Abstract International*, Vol. 56, No. 2, August (1995), p. 512A.

Gallagher, D.J. (2001). Neutrality as a moral standpoint, conceptual confusion and the full inclusion debate. *Disability and Society*, Vol. 16, No. 5, pp. 637-654.

Gash, H. and Coffey, I. (1995). Influences on attitudes towards children with mental handicap. *European Journal of Special Needs Education*, Vol. 10, No. 1, pp. 1-16.

Gash, H. (1996). Changing attitudes towards children with special needs. *European Journal of Special Needs Education*, Vol. II, No. 3, pp. 286-297.

Giangreco, M.F., Edelman, S.W. and Broer, S.M. (2001). Respect, appreciation and acknowledgement of para-professionals who support students with disabilities. *The Council for Exceptional Children*, Vol. 67, No. 4, pp. 485-498.

Golby, M. and Gulliver, R.J. (1985). Whose remedies, whose ills? *Journal of Curriculum Studies*, Vol. 11, No. 2.

Grainger, T., Tod, J. and Fox, R. (2001). Inclusive educational practice: Literacy. *Reading*, Vol. 35, No. 3.

Herman, J.E. (1995). The adaptation of regular elementary classrooms for children with moderate and severe disabilities: Inclusion practices from the principal's perspective. *Dissertation Abstracts International*, Vol. 56, No. 4, p. 1315A.

Heward, W.L. (1996). *Exceptional Children: An Introduction to Special Education* (5th ed.). Columbus, OH Merrill.

Hewett, F.M. and Forness, S.R. (1984). *Education of Exceptional Children*. London, Allyn & Bacon.

Hofman, R.H. (1999). Contribution of clusters to integration. *European Journal of Special Needs Education,* Vol. 14, No. 3, pp. 187-197.

Hornby, G. and Kdd, R. (2001). Transfer from special to mainstream ten years later. *British Journal of Special Education,* Vol. 28, No. 1, pp. 10-17.

Husen, T. and Neville, P.T. (1985). *The International Encyclopedia of Education*. New York, Pergamon Publication.

Iyanar, J. (2001). Listening to different voices—Inclusion and inclusion of people with disabilities in education. *Asia Pacific Disability Rehabilitation Journal,* Vol. 12, No. 2, pp. 155-159.

Johnson, T. (1995). *Inclusive Education*. Geneva, UNDP.

Julka, A. (2001). Concept of inclusive education. *In Self-learning Materials on National Curriculum Framework for School Education and Education of Special Focused Groups*. New Delhi, NCERT, p. 4.

Karagiannis, A. (1994). The waves of special education over the last two hundred years: Significance and implication for inclusive schools. Paper presented at the Excellence and Equity in Education, International Conference, Toronto.

Karagiannis, A. (1996). Rationale for inclusive schooling. In S. Stainback, and W. Stainback, (eds.) *Inclusion: A Guide for Educators*. London, Paul H. Brookes.

Kauffman, J.M. and Hallahan, D.P. (1978). *Exceptional Children: Introduction to Special Education*. New Jersey, Prentice Hall.

Kohli, T. (2002). *Workshop on Inclusive Education*. Punjab University, Chandigarh.

Lacey, P. (2001). The role of learning support assistances in the inclusive learning of pupils with special educational needs. *Educational Review,* Vol. 53, No. 2.

Lembo, J.M. (1971). *Why Teachers Fail.* Columbus, Merrill.

Lindsay, G. (2003). Inclusive education: A critical perspective. *British Journal of Special Education,* Vol. 30, No. 1, pp. 3-12.

Lioyd, J.W. (1988). Direct academic interventions in learning disabilities. In M.C. Wang, M.C. Reynolds and H.J. Walberg (eds.) *Handbook of Special Education: Research and Practice,* Vol. 2, Oxford, Pergamon.

Lipsky, D.K. and Gartner, A. (1994). Inclusion: What it is, what it is not, and why it matters. *Exceptional Parents.* September, p. 36.

Loreman, T. and Deppeler, J.M. (2001). Working towards full inclusion in education in access. *The National Issues Journal for People with a Disability.* Vol. 3(6), pp. 5-8.

Loreman, T. Deppeler, J. and Harvey, D. (2005). *Inclusive Education: A Practical Guide to Supporting Diversity in the Classroom.* Routledge Falmer, London.

Maheswari, P. and Raina, K. (1998). Interactive video technology in professional development of teachers. *Defining Quality in Education,* Paris, UNICEF.

Mani, M.N.G. (1999). UNESCO International Institute for Special Education. Proposal submitted to the UNESCO and Government of India.

Mani, C. (1988). *The Physically Handicapped in India.* New Delhi, Ashish Publishing Ltd.

Mc. Gregor, G. and Vogelsberg, R.T. (1998). Inclusive schooling practices: Pedagogical and research foundation, Baltimore, Paul H. Brookes.

Meyen, E.L. (1996). *Exceptional Children in Today's School* (3rd ed.). Love, Denver.

Miles, M. (1997). *Disability, Care and Education in the 19th Century India: Some Dates, Places and Documentation* (ERIC documents, No. 408747). New Delhi, NCERT.

Miske, D. and et al. (1998). Rate of attendance, learning gains and rate of repetition: A study of village-based schools in Malawi. *Defining Quality in Education.* Paris, UNICEF.

Mukherjee, S. (2000). The inclusion of pupils with a chronic health condition in mainstream school: What does it mean for teachers? *Educational Research*, Vol. 42, No. 1, pp. 59-72.

Namibian Case Study of Inclusiveness in the Classroom (2000). *Education Today: The Newsletter of UNESCO's Education Sector*, October-December, 2003, No. 7, Paris.

O' Reilly, F.E. (2000). Getting in and staying in: A longitudinal study of student placement and persistence in inclusionary settings. *Dissertation Abstract International*, Vol. 61, No. 10, p. 3953.

Palmer, D.S. and Aroha, T. (2001). Taking sides: Parent views on inclusion for three children with severe disabilities. *The Council for Exceptional Children*, Vol. 67, No. 4, pp. 467-484.

Pandey, R.S. and Advani, L. (1997). *Perspectives in Disability and Rehabilitation*. New Delhi, Vikash Publications.

Pickett, R.C. (1993). The relationship between school structure, culture and student views of diversity and inclusive education: A comparative case study of two middle schools. *Dissertation Abstracts International*, Vol. 54, No. 7, p. 2537A.

Pressley, M. and Mc Cormick, C.B. (1995). *Advanced Educational Psychology for Educators, Researchers and Policy-makers*. New York, Harper Collins.

PWD Act (1995). In CRE programme organized by Prof. Tehl Kohli from 18th to 22nd January 2005 sponsored by RCI in INPA, Karuna Sadan, Chandigarh.

Rane, A.J. (1983). Integrated education of disabled children: An evaluation of the scheme of integrated education for handicapped children based on a study of the working of the scheme in Maharastra. In M.B. Buch (1991) *Fourth Survey of Research in Education (1983-88)*, Vol. II, New Delhi, NCERT.

Rao, I. (2003). Inclusive education in the Indian context. Paper presented in the training of key persons. New Delhi, NCERT (from 16th-17th September 2003).

Rao, S. (2001). 'A Little Inconvenience': Perspectives of Bengali families of children with disabilities on labeling and inclusion. *Disability and Society,* Vol. 16. No. 4, pp. 531-548.

Rauchak, D.P. and Eggen, P.D. (1998). *Learning and Teaching: Research-based Methods* (3rd ed.). Boston, Allyn & Bacon.

Redding, N. (2000). Family support for learning. *Defining Quality in Education.* Paris, UNICEF.

Rehabilitation Council of India (1996). *9th Annual Report* (1995-96). New Delhi, RCI.

Ricciato, D. (2000). Teacher perceptions regarding new knowledge needed for inclusion of children with severe multiple disabilities. *Dissertation Abstracts International,* Vol. 61, No. 2, p. 567.

Santos, M. (2001). Inclusion and/or integration: The debate is still in Brazil. *Disability and Society,* Vol. 16, No. 6, pp. 893-897.

Sarva Shiksha Abhiyan (2002). Education for All. Guidelines of the Government of India.

Schaffner, C.B. and Buswell, B.E. (1996). Ten critical elements for creating inclusive and effective school communities. In S. Stainback, and W. Stainback (eds.) *Inclusion: A Guide for Educators.* London: Paul. H. Brookes.

Schaffner, C.B. and Buswell, B.E. (1991). *Opening Doors: Strategies for Including All Students in Regular Education.* Colorado, Springs: PEAK Parent Center Inc.

Schwartz, C. and Armony-Slvan, R. (2001). Students' attitudes to the inclusion of people with disabilities in the community. *Disability and Society,* Vol. 16, No. 3, pp. 403-413.

Schwartz, S.E. and Karge, B.D. (1996). *Human Diversity: A Guide for Understanding* (2nd ed.). London, McGraw-Hill.

Sebba, J. and Ainseow, M. (1996). International developments in inclusive schooling: Mapping the issues. *Cambridge Journal of Education,* Vol. 26, No. 1.

Shevlin, M. (2003). Preparing for contract between mainstream pupils and their counterparts who have severe and profound and multiple learning disabilities. *British Journal of Special Education,* Vol. 30, No. 2, pp. 93-99.

Sigmon, S. (1983). The history and future of educational segregation. *Journal for Special Education,* Vol. 19, pp. 1-13.

Sindelar, P.T., Griffin, C.C., Smith, S.W., and Watanabe, A.K. (1992). Prereferral intervention: Encouraging notes on preliminary findings. *The Elementary School Journal,* Vol. 9, No. 3, pp. 245-259.

Singh, R.P. and Prabha, S. (1987). Education of integrated educational facilities for physically handicapped in the schools of Bihar. In M.B. Buch (1991) *Fourth Survey of Research in Education* (1983-88), Vol. II, New Delhi, NCERT.

Singh, S. (2001). Educational needs, relevant curriculum and rehabilitational expectations of handicapped children. *Indian Educational Review,* Vol. 37, No. 1, pp. 85-90.

Slee, R. (2001). "Inclusion in practice.": Does practice make perfect? *Educational Review,* Vol. 53, No. 2.

Smith, T.C., Polloway, E.A., Patton, J.R. and Dowdy, C.A. (2nd ed) (1996). *Teaching Students with Special Needs in Inclusive Setting.* Boston, Allyn & Bacon.

Soni, R.B.L. (2002). Pupils' attitudes toward integration and friendship in New Delhi. *Indian Educational Review,* Vol. 38, No. 1, pp. 86-89.

Soni, R.B.L. (2000). Mainstreaming of the handicapped. *The Primary Teacher.* April, pp. 69-79.

Stainback, S. and Stainback, W. (1990). *Support Networks for Inclusive Schooling: Interdependent Integrated Education.* Baltimore, Paul Brookes, pp. 1-56.

Stainback, S. and Stainback, W. (1989). *Inclusion: A Guide for Educators.* Baltimore, Pauls Brookes.

Stainback, S., Stainback, W. and Forest, M. (1989). *Educating All Students in the Mainstream of Regular Education.* Baltimore, Paul Brookes.

The Salamanca Statement and Framework for Action on Special Needs Education (1994). Presentation at the World Conference on Special Needs Education: Access and Quality at Salamanca, 1994.

Thomas, G. (1997). Inclusive schools for an inclusive society. *British Journal of Special Education,* Vol. 24, No. 3, pp. 103-106.

Thomas, G., Walker, D. and Webb, J. (1998). *The Making of the Inclusive School.* Routledge, London.

Thomas, G., Walker, D. and Webb, J. (1998). In John Wilson (2000). Doing justice to inclusion. *European Journal of Special Needs Education,* Vol. 15, No. 3, pp. 297-304.

Topping, K.J. (1998). *The Peer-tutoring Handbook: Promoting Cooperating Learning.* Croom Helm, London.

Turn-kaspa, H., Weisel, A. and Most, T. (2000). A multi-dimensional study of special education students' attitudes toward people with disabilities: A focus on deafness. *European Journal of Special Needs Education,* Vol. 15, No. 1, pp. 13-23.

Udvari-Solner, A. and Thousand, A. (1995). Effective organizational instructional and curricular practices in inclusive schools and classrooms. In C. Clark, A. Dyson and A. Millward (eds.) *Towards Inclusive Schools.* London, Fulton.

UNICEF (1998). *Report on Early Childhood Programmes for Disadvantaged Children.* Paris.

UNICEF (2000). *Defining Quality in Education.* Paris.

Vandercook, T., Fleetham, D., Sinclair, S. and Tetlie, R. (1988). Cath, Jess, Jules, and Ames A story of friendship. *IMPACT,* Vol. 2, pp. 18-19.

Vandercook, T., York, J. and Forest, M. (1989). *MAPS: A Strategy for Building a Vision.* Minneapolis, Institute on Community Integration.

Verma, J. (2000). Towards achieving the target of education for all. *The Primary Teacher.* April, pp. 88-91.

Vislie, L. (2003). From integration to inclusion: Focusing global trends and changes in the Western European societies. *European Journal of Special Needs Education,* Vol. 18, No. 1, pp. 12-17.

Wade, B., More, M. and Berdousi, E. (1995). Education in Greek special units: What Greek pupils with special educational needs tell us about their schooling. *European Journal of Special Education,* Vol. 10, No. 1, pp. 17-30.

Ware, L. (1995). The aftermath of the articulate debate: The invention of inclusive education. In C. Clark and et al. (eds.) *Towards Inclusive School.* London, Fulton.

Warnock, B.M. (1978). In Paul Croll and Diana Moses (2000), Ideologies & Utopias: Education professionals' views of inclusion. *European Journal of Special Needs Education,* Vol. 15, No. 1, pp. 1-12.

Wehman, P. (1990). School to work: Elements of successful programme. *Teaching Exceptional Children,* Vol. 23, pp. 40.

Westwood, P. (1998). Reducing educational failure. *Australian Journal of Learning Disabilities,* Vol. 3, No. 3, pp. 4-12.

Westwood, P.S. (1997). *Commonsense Methods for Children with Special Needs* (3rd ed.). London, Routledge.

Wiersama, W. (1986). *Research Methods in Education: An Introduction* (4th ed.). Toronto, Allyn & Bacan Inc.

Willms, P. (2000). Early childhood psycho-social development experiences in Latin American countries. *Defining Quality in Education,* Paris, UNICEF.

Wilson, J. (2000). Doing justice to inclusion. *European Journal of Special Needs Education,* Vol. 15, No. 3, pp. 297-304.

Yeager, N.S. (1994). Analysis of absenteeism: Achievement and self-concept of elementary students in an inclusive classroom. *Dissertation Abstract International,* Vol. 56, No. 4, October (1995), p. 1317A.

On-line References

Ainscow, M. (2004). A one-day workshop: Developing effective schools for all.
www.ied.edu.hk/csnsie/program.html.

Ainscow, M. (2004). Developing inclusive practices in schools. ***www.ied.edu.hk/csnsie/program.html.***

Ainscow, M. (2004). Reaching out to all learners: How can classrooms be made more inclusive?
www.ied.edu.hk/csnsie/program.html.

Alper, S. (1995). Inclusion: Preparing for inclusion what role can administrators play in inclusive education? ***www.uni.edu/coeinclusion/preparing/administrators.html.***

Barrafato, A. (1998). Supports and resources, parental and teacher attitude, in-service training and planning contribute to the successful inclusion of children with disabilities at the early childhood level. *Dissertation Abstract International*. ***www.lib.umi.com/dissertations/search.***

Brown, T.T. (1998). Middle school personnel's attitudes towards inclusive education in a suburban Texas school district. *Dissertation Abstract International*. ***www.lib.umi.com/dissertations/search.***

Daack, E.E. (1999). Preparing for inclusion. ***www.uni.edu/coe/inclusion/preparing_levels.html.***

Daack, E.E. (1999). Preparing for inclusion: Inclusion models for a building level. ***www.uni.edu/ ioe/inclusion/preparing/ building_levels.html.***

Francis, D. and Muthukrishna, N. (2004). Able voice on inclusion/exclusion people in their own words. *International Journal of Special Education*, Vol.19, No.1. ***www.internationaljournalofspecialeducation.com.***

Gorne, L.A. (1997). Quality indicators in inclusive education. *Dissertation Abstract International*. ***www.lib.umi.com/dissertations/search.***

Hill, M. (2000). Relationship between teacher beliefs and inclusive education. *Dissertation Abstract International*. ***www.liabrary.puchd.ac.in.***

Horton, C. (1998). Opinions of parents of both disabled and non-disabled elementary school children regarding inclusion of disabled students in regular education classes. *Dissertation Abstract International*. ***www.lib.umi.com/dissertations/search.***

Inclusive education: Capacity building and resource development for the promotion of basic education for focusing on minimizing marginalization and exclusion. ***www.unescobkk.org/education/appeal/topic08.htm.***

Inclusive education in the region: Addressing marginalization and exclusion in basic education. ***www.unescbkk.org/ips/ebooks/documents/appealbulletin 10-1/5inclusive.pdf.***

Inclusive education: The salmanca statement and framework for action on special needs education, para 3. ***www.unescobkk.org/education/appeal/topic08.htm.***

Inclusive science and special educational needs. ***www.isn/net/~jypsy/education/html.***

Jha, M. (1997). A study on management pattern of integrated and special school for the disabled in Bihar. ***www.lib.umi.com/dissertations/search.***

Koshy, A. (2003). Inclusive Training in Schools. ***www.wed.utk.edu/%7Ejece/facultymain.html.***

Leong, K.T. and Kooi, S.W. (2004). Thoughtful strategies for inclusive classrooms in Brunei Darussalan. *International Journal of Special Education*, Vol. 19, No. 2. ***www.international journal of special education.com.***

Mani, M.N.G. (2003). Inclusive education in India: Policies and practices. *The Educator*, January-June. ***www.icevi.org/publications/educator/June-03/article24 htm.***

Manivnan, M. (2003). Inclusive education for disabled children. ***web.utk.edu/facultymain.html.index/.shtmlindex/.shtml.***

Maricle M. (2001). A study on attitudes of New Jersey public secondary school principals toward inclusive education and educational strategies related to its practice. ***www.lib.umi.com/dissertations/search.***

Meijer, C.J.W. (2002). Inclusive education and classroom practices: European agency for development in special needs education. ***www.edu.file.rityiso-petus/agency/inclusive.nov.2002pdf.***

Mendez, G. (1998). The effect of teachers' perceived self-efficacy, beliefs and subsequent behaviours and support for research-based effective teaching behaviours on their attitudes toward children with special needs: Implications for inclusive education. *Dissertation Abstract International.* ***www.lib.umi.com/dissertations/search.***

Miles, S. (2003). Educational support and inclusion. ***E-mail: info@eenet.org.uk.***

Moran, A. and Abott, L. (2002). Developing inclusive schools: The pivotal role of teaching assistances in promoting inclusion in special and mainstream schools in Northern

Ireland. *European Journal of Special Needs Education*, Vol. 17, No. 2, pp. 161-173.
www.educationarena.com/educationsarena/sample/sample-pdf.

Myreddi, V. and Narayan, J. (2003). Preparation of special education teachers' present status and future trends. ***www.wed.utk.edu/%7Eiece/facultymain.html.***

Naidu, P. (2000). Head start teachers' conceptions of full inclusion of young children. *Dissertation Abstract International.*
www.library.puchd.ac.in.

National Policy on Education (1986). Department of Education, Government of India.
www.education.nic.in/html/web/natpol.html#1.

Norwich, B. (2000). Can effective schools be inclusive schools? University of Exeter.
www.literacytrust.org.uk/Database/enupdate.html/#inclusive.

O'Hanlon, C. (2001). Learning from research: Influence on successful inclusion strategies.
www.ied.education.hk/csnsie/program.htm.

O'Hanlon, C. (2003). Educational inclusion as action research. ***www.ied.edu hk/csnsie/program.htm.***

Ofsted (2004). Mainstream schools are failing to make progress.
www.literacytrust.org.uk/Database/senupdate.html/#inclusive.

Papadopoulou, D., Kokaridas, D., Papanikolaou, Z., and Patsiaoura, A. (2004). Attitudes of Greek physical education teachers toward inclusion of students with disabilities. *International Journal of Special Education*, Vol. 19, No. 2.
www.Internationaljournalofspecialeducation.com.

Renaissance Group (1999). Philosophy of inclusive education. ***www.uni.edu/coe/inclusion/philoso-phy/philosophy.html.***

Renaissance Group (2004). Inclusion-teaching strategies. ***www.uni.edu/coe/inclusion/strategies/content-behaviour.html.***

Rustemier, S. (2003). Inclusive education: A worldwide movement.
www.utk.edu.%7Eiece/facultymain.html.

Sarva Shiksha Abhiyan. Department of Education, Government of India.
www.education.nic.in/html.

Treder, D.W. (1998). Teacher effectiveness and teacher attitudes toward children with special needs: Implications for inclusive education. *Dissertation Abstract International.*
www.lib.umi.com/dissertations/search.

Tuli, U. (2000). Challenges of inclusive education. E-mail: ***amarjoti@del.***
www.dissertationsandtheses.com.

Westwood, C.A.C. (2002). The successful inclusion of children with emotional and behavioural disorders into general education settings. *International Journal of Disability, Community and Rehabilitation*, Vol. 1, No. 3.
www.ijdcr.ca/VOL01_03_CAN/index.shtml

Wills, S. (2000). A study on the effects of government restructuring on inclusive education—Perceptions of educators in a school division in Alberta.
www.library.puchd.ac.in.

Zahn, G.D. (1998). Perceptions and attitudes of elementary school teachers toward the practice of inclusion, its implementation, impact and future. *Dissertation Abstract International.*
www.lib.umi.com/dissertations/search.

Subject Index